# Buttermilk and Bible Burgers

Endowed by

**Tom Watson Brown**

*and*

**The Watson-Brown Foundation, Inc.**

# FRED SAUCEMAN

# BUTTERMILK & BIBLE BURGERS

## more stories from the kitchens of appalachia

Mercer University Press • Macon, Georgia

MUP/481

2014 Mercer University Press

1400 Coleman Avenue

Macon, Georgia 31207

First Edition

Book design by Burt&Burt

Books published by Mercer University Press are printed on
acid-free paper that meets the requirements of the American National Standard
for Information Sciences–Permanence of Paper for Printed Library Materials.

Mercer University Press is a member of Green Press Initiative (greenpressinitiative.org),
a nonprofit organization working to help publishers and printers increase their use of recycled paper
and decrease their use of fiber derived from endangered forests. This book is printed on recycled paper.

ISBN 978-0-88146-479 5

Library of Congress Cataloging-in-Publication Data

Sauceman, Fred William.
Buttermilk and Bible burgers : more stories from the kitchens of Appalachia / Fred W. Sauceman. – First edition.
pages cm
Includes index.
ISBN 978-0-88146-479-5 (paperback : alkaline paper)  ISBN 0-88146-479-1 (paperback : alkaline paper)
1. Food habits – Appalachian Region, Southern. 2. Cooking – Appalachian Region, Southern.
3. Restaurants – Appalachian Region, Southern. 4. Appalachian Region, Southern – Social life and customs.
5. Appalachian Region, Southern – Biography. 6. Appalachian Region, Southern – History, Local.
7. Sauceman, Fred William – Travel – Appalachian Region, Southern. 8. Appalachian Region, Southern – Description and travel.
I. Title.
GT2853.U5S28 2014    394.1'2 – dc23
2014002539

Part Two

# THE PRODUCTS

Part Three

# THE PLACES

# PREFACE

## Appalachia Is...

Appalachia is a coffee can of bacon grease sitting by the stove, both convenient and defiant.

Appalachia is a slab of Allan Benton's bacon washed down with a swig of Earl Cruze's buttermilk.

Appalachia is redeye gravy, a two-toned reminder of hard times.

Appalachia is a noontime, creekbank dinner of potted meat, Vienna sausage, and Nehi in between bluegill strikes.

Appalachia is country-fried steak at a Ruritan Club.

Appalachia is the taste of sunshine in a Cherokee purple tomato.

Appalachia is Ale-8-One in Kentucky, Grapico in Alabama, and Dr. Enuf in Tennessee.

Appalachia is dry-land fish: morel mushrooms foraged from a secret patch in April, dipped in egg and buttermilk, rolled in cornmeal, and fried.

Appalachia is the world's most adaptable measurement: a mess. A mess of greens, a mess of okra, a mess of beans. Enough to feed your family, or anybody else who happens by.

Appalachia is brains and eggs.

Appalachia is poetry on a plate: Greasy Beans and Silver Queen and Better Boys.

Appalachia is killed lettuce and the mystic chemistry of vinegar and pork fat.

Appalachia is digging ramps at 3,200 feet and a hands-and-knees sip at the mouth of a mountain spring.

Appalachia is the politics of pepperoni rolls.

Appalachia is the infinite variety of the deviled egg, the infinite variety of the plates that cradle them, and the infinite variety of churches that nurture them.

Appalachia is a bowl of blue cheese dressing and a corona of saltines at Ridgewood Barbecue in Bluff City, Tennessee.

*Appalachian Mountains and rhododendrons along the Appalachian Trail. Photo by Dave Allen Photo/BigStock.*

Appalachia is the barnyard wisdom of Ridgewood's founder, the late Grace Proffitt: Stay with the pig until he makes a hog.

Appalachia is slugburgers in Mississippi and Arvil Burgers in Tennessee.

Appalachia is a batter-dunked, deep-fried, mustard-painted Dip Dog on the Lee Highway in Virginia.

Appalachia is pure sugar stick candy at Christmastime, in a stark white box with a red stripe.

Appalachia is a pork chop sandwich at the Snappy Lunch in Mount Airy, North Carolina, leaking out mustard, onions, tomato, slaw, and sugar-sweetened chili.

Appalachia is a Wormy Steak at a place the gutsy owners call the Grease Rack in Newport, Tennessee.

Appalachia is a memory of cottage cheese croquettes from Sophronia Strong Hall cafeteria at the University of Tennessee.

Appalachia is Harold and Addie Shersky working elbow to elbow for over fifty-five years at Harold's Kosher-style Deli in Knoxville, Tennessee.

Appalachia is a vehement argument over chicken and dumplings: rolled dough or dropped dough, puffy or flat.

Appalachia is the great biscuit continuum: angel biscuits on one end; beaten biscuits their polar opposite.

Appalachia is sustainable without saying it.

Appalachia is Beans All the Way.

Appalachia is the permanence of a black-iron skillet.

This book is a personal portrait of my Appalachia.

# ACKNOWLEDGMENTS

I OFFER A SWEET TEA TOAST TO THE STAFF AT MERCER UNIVERSITY PRESS IN MACON, Georgia—most especially Dr. Marc Jolley, Marsha Luttrell, and Jenny Toole—for believing in my work, all the way back to our chance encounter in Memphis, Tennessee, in 2004. This is the fourth book we have done together. Each one has been a joy.

Since I was fifteen years old, when I landed my first job in radio, I have enjoyed the company of people who make their living as media professionals. To those who have afforded me outlets to share my stories of the people of Appalachia and their foodways, I extend special thanks: John Molley, Jan Hearne, and the staff of the *Johnson City Press* in Tennessee; Tim Cable, Melissa Hipolit, Shira Evans, Josh Smith, and the staff at

*Caramel cake
by Linda Smith.
Photo by Larry Smith.*

WJHL-TV in Johnson City; Beth Vorhees, producer of West Virginia Public Broadcasting's *Inside Appalachia*; Kurt Rheinheimer and the staff of *Blue Ridge Country* magazine, headquartered in Roanoke, Virginia; and Mary Constantine with the *Knoxville News Sentinel*.

Larry Smith, director of Photographic Services at East Tennessee State University, and I have worked together since spring 1985. His photographic talents honor the land and the people of Appalachia in a grand way.

I am fortunate to be able to work, every day, with a team of talented people in the Division of University Relations, at the Center for Appalachian Studies and Services, and at WETS-FM/HD, all on the campus of East Tennessee State University, where I have been rewardingly employed since 1985.

The people who have so openly shared their stories with me deserve the highest credit for this book, as well as the three volumes of the *Place Setting* series that accompany it. I appreciate their candor, their humor, their honesty, their dedication, and the lessons they teach through food.

Finally, and most important, I thank my wife Jill, a full partner in my exploration of our homeland in Southern Appalachia. Although she is not the kind of person who seeks notoriety, she has earned it. Our most requested recipe, by far, is one she rescued. She learned to make dried apple stack cake in her grandmother's kitchen in Scott County, Virginia, and she has shared that recipe widely. It is profound in its simplicity and frugality and a fitting and flavorful symbol for our beloved region.

Grateful acknowledgment is made to the following for permission to reprint previously published material: the *Johnson City Press*; *Blue Ridge Country* magazine; *Our State* magazine; *The Encyclopedia of Alabama*; and *Now & Then: The Appalachian Magazine*.

BUTTERMILK &
BIBLE BURGERS

PART ONE
THE PEOPLE

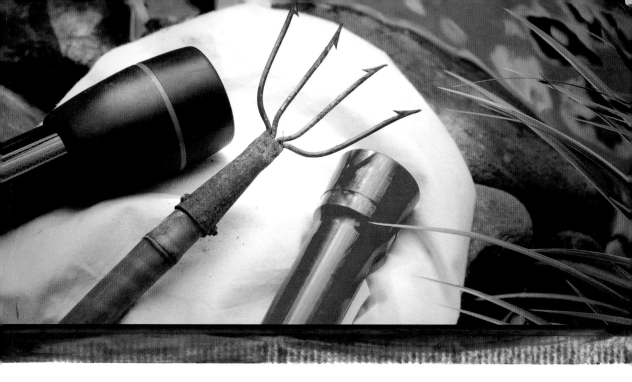

# A SIXTIES SUMMERTIME MEMORY OF FROG HUNTING

**I DON'T HEAR MUCH TALK OF FROG-HUNTING ANYMORE.** Biologists say the frog population is declining worldwide, an ominous sign for the planet and its ecosystems. And today, the conditions under which my father and I hunted frogs in the 1960s would be dangerous if not possibly fatal.

Back then, my father thought nothing about showing up in the middle of the night, unannounced, on the banks of someone's farm pond in rural Greene County, Tennessee. The Magnavox Company, where he worked, employed about 6,000 people in the 1960s, and he knew just about all of them. Many of his coworkers lived out in the county, and they had ponds.

My father never felt it necessary to call ahead or even go up to an owner's house, knock on the door, and announce our presence. Yet we were never confronted, accosted, or fired upon. Think of it. Two truck headlights scan the fields, a lit cigarette is traceable from truck to pond, a flashlight draws patterns on the water's surface and, if my attention lapses, on the clouds above. Despite the light show, nobody gets suspicious.

We completed these hunts without interruptions from any anxious landowners, ever. Grasping a cane pole with a gig attached, my father

*Flashlights, a cotton sack, and a gig: tools of the frog-hunting trade. Photo by Larry Smith.*

would tiptoe around the water's edge while I held the flashlight and a cotton sack. That was my assignment: circling strange ponds for hours late at night, blinding amphibians. When my beam of light met two eyes just above the water line, my father, rocking back on one foot like a javelin thrower, would spear the frog with that gig.

Primitive, perhaps. But the alternative was rifle fire: .22-caliber hollow-point bullets. They greatly increased your range, certainly. But wading into the cold, dark, snaky water without the luxury of hip boots to try to retrieve the frog negated the advantage.

Most every hardware store carried frog gigs in those days. They consisted of four barbed prongs. A good supply of cane poles always stood in the corner of our garage. We made teepee structures out of them for beans to climb on in the summertime. And they were my fishing poles. There were no mechanical parts on my childhood fishing gear. No reels. No line entanglement. Not much casting, really. Cane poles were versatile tools at our house.

Toward midnight, when the cotton sack got so heavy and so jumpy with frogs that I could barely carry it, we'd head back home, and my father would clean the frogs in the backyard. The implements were always the same: a block of concrete, a yellow Case pocketknife, a pair of pliers, and a pan of water.

In 2009, for a special foodways issue, the staff at the University of North Carolina's *Southern Cultures* magazine asked me to write a short piece about my favorite food. I contemplated country ham, fried chicken, rice with gravy, oysters, and soup beans. But, as much for the memory as the taste, I settled on fresh frog legs. Freeze them, and the flavor, texture, and color are lost. Fresh out of the pond, they are ethereal.

The morning after those frog hunts, my mother would roll the legs in salted and peppered flour and fry them lightly in a black iron skillet. The cotton-white meat is still my favorite food, the recollection of it made all the more poignant because these trips into the night were cut short too early by my father's untimely death in the winter of 1973.

I haven't frog-hunted since.

# A GRANDMOTHER'S GIFT OF FOOD

**MILK SO COLD THAT IT WAS CRUNCHY WITH ICE CRYSTALS.** The interplay of popcorn and roasted peanuts. An angel food cake cooling in its pan and mounted on a Coke bottle, like a crown.

They are flavors from a lost world. Grandmother food. Of my maternal grandmother's kitchen handiwork, I remember only a few sit-down-at-the-table dishes.

What stands out more clearly is the little-boy food, the between-meal creations intended not so much to satisfy hunger as to please a grandson. My grandmother, Edith Ethel Koontz Royall, knew exactly the right temperature to ice the milk without freezing it. She knew just when to remove the popcorn popper from the heat so the peanuts were pleasantly parched, not scorched. She knew how to add just enough bread to stretch her hamburger meat into a pleasant, peppery softness.

*My maternal grandmother, Edith Ethel Koontz Royall.*

Kitchen technique wasn't the only thing she mastered in her lifetime. Born on March 6, 1894, in Afton, Tennessee, she learned to drive a car in an era when not many rural women in her part of the country had the chance to pick up that skill. She worked outside the home as a telephone switchboard operator while her husband was protecting the Town of Greeneville as Night Chief of Police.

Despite their odd, sometimes out-of-synch schedules, they raised three children. My grandmother and my grandfather, William Franklin Royall, were night-and-day different. When it came to food, she had no hang-ups. But he had a phobia of egg whites. Shaped by the Depression as she was, my grandmother turned his dislike into a sort of cottage industry. With my grandfather eating only the yolks of his eggs, she would collect the whites, bake angel food cakes, and sell them for a dollar each on the streets of their neighborhood in Greeneville in the 1930s.

Otherwise calm and quiet, my grandmother was a torrent in the kitchen. She was known for her monumental messes. She prepared the meals. She expected others to deal with the aftermath.

In her final years, her labors ended by strokes and a failing heart, kinfolks brought the food to her. March 6 meant coconut cake and boiled custard and the Wesley Blessing, its words etched into a family heirloom teapot.

Even though her own kitchen duty ended some six years before her death in 1971, my grandmother never lost interest in cooking. She was a faithful fan of Mary Starr, host of the *Homemakers' Show* on WATE-TV, channel 6, in Knoxville. In fact, when my grandmother recalled, verbatim, a Mary Starr potato soup recipe from the television show, we knew that she had overcome her stroke.

To celebrate my grandmother's life, we stuff peppers. The ingredients hearken back to a Greene County farm from long ago: tomatoes, onions, whole-hog sausage, and leftover biscuits. The method reveals my grandmother's wisdom and frugality. For its nutrients and flavor, she insisted, the water you boil the green peppers in must be saved. Despite the intervening years, it's a lesson in character and in cooking that I've never forgotten.

 ## Grandmother Royall's Stuffed Peppers

6 green bell peppers, cut in half with seeds, stem, and membrane removed

1 package stuffing mix or the equivalent amount of toasted leftover biscuits or cornbread

3 ears fresh corn, removed from the cob

2 tomatoes, chopped

1 onion, chopped

Season to taste with any combination of oregano, sage, chili powder, salt, and pepper

1 pound sausage, fried, crumbled, and drained of grease

12 slices cheddar cheese

*Parboil the peppers briefly and save the pepper water. Mix stuffing or bread with corn, tomatoes, onion, seasonings, and sausage. Add enough pepper water to make a moist mixture. Grease a baking dish and pour a little pepper water in the bottom. Stuff the peppers and cover each with a slice of cheddar cheese. Cover with foil and bake at 350 degrees for about 45 minutes, uncovering for the last 10 minutes so the cheese can brown slightly.*

*Trula Bailey offers up
one of her wholewheat
muffins. Watercolor by
Nancy Jane Earnest.*

# REMEMBERING TRULA BAILEY

**HER NAME WAS ALMOST MUSICAL.** Trula Bailey. Her falsetto laugh would get you every time. But what she could do with a frying pan and a bowl of flour was almost miraculous.

I'm sure she fed me my first mushroom. My fascination with eggplant began with her. And to this day, over thirty years later, I still say she made the prettiest pie I've ever seen, an apricot chiffon.

I suppose some would have called Trula Bailey a domestic. I never used that word. Although she worked for my aunt and uncle, Mary Nelle and Grover Graves, in Athens, Tennessee, for decades, to them it was never much of an employer-employee relationship. Trula did the kinds of things people in white uniforms did in the 1950s and '60s. She cooked. She cleaned. But above all the chores, she cared.

Trula needed a family. She never had much luck with men. "I'm going to divide your head," she reportedly said once to her husband after he had been out all night.

She remained childless. After her mother died, a blind sister was her only relative. It was the Graves family, white and well off, that shaped her world. While my uncle ran the First National Bank and my aunt worked in the President's Office at Tennessee Wesleyan College, Trula oversaw operations on the home front, 102 Forrest Avenue.

To the duties of running a busy household, she added the responsibilities of a self-taught health care pro, helping my grandmother learn to walk and talk and write again after a devastating stroke.

Trula always spoke with a smile in her voice. With the exception of encounters involving errant spouses, most of her stories were happy ones.

She had grown up in Vonore, with both Cherokee and African American ancestry. My uncle's first wife taught her to read in the 1930s. Equipped with that new skill, Trula scoured cookbooks, magazines, and newspapers and combined the trendy with the tried-and-true, coming up with a cooking style all her own.

Take the whole-wheat muffins she made for my uncle's two sons, who stuffed them into their pockets and headed off for school. She built such a reputation in Athens with those muffins that folks began calling them "Trula Rolls."

Yet no one could replicate them. In her later years, I attempted to document the recipe. I never believed that Trula was being less than forthcoming with me by withholding an ingredient, but I could never match her results.

In *Ford Times*, a small magazine published by the motor company, Trula noticed an eggplant recipe and fashioned it as her own: Stuffed Eggplant on the Half Shell. Its Ritz cracker topping and silver knife doneness test speak of the 1950s. We still make it today.

Trula could take a piece of round steak, some flour, some oil, and salt and pepper and make gravy with a flavor so deep, you'd swear she'd emptied the spice shelf.

Trula took most of her meals alone in the Graves kitchen, and when guests wanted seconds, which they invariably did, my aunt would ring a bell for service. But as civil rights advances occurred in the 1960s, that bell was eventually put away, and Trula finally claimed her rightful spot at the long wooden table in the family dining room.

That house, once filled with the smell of baking country hams and bourbon-laced sweet potatoes, is no longer in the family. The last meal I had there was more than fifteen years ago. Most of the people who sat around that table and celebrated my grandmother's birthday every March 6 with coconut cake and boiled custard are gone.

Trula was one of the last to go. She died on January 6, 2002, at age ninety-two, and is buried in Athens alongside her mother, sister, and that husband she once threatened.

Now, on our dining room wall in Johnson City hangs a watercolor, painted by Nancy Earnest, from a photograph. It's Trula, breaking into a big smile and offering up one of her enigmatic whole-wheat muffins once again.

## Trula Bailey's Stuffed Eggplant on the Half Shell

| | |
|---|---|
| 1 | large eggplant, split lengthwise |
| | Salt and pepper to taste |
| 1 | cup celery, chopped |
| 1/4 | cup onion, chopped |
| 3 | ounces butter |
| 2 | eggs, well beaten |
| 1 | cup milk |
| 1/2 | cup grated sharp cheddar cheese |
| 1 | cup Ritz crackers, rolled, plus extra for topping |

*Scoop insides from eggplant and cook in salt water until tender. Drain, chop, and season with salt and pepper. Cook celery and onion in butter until tender. Mix with seasoned eggplant and remaining ingredients and place in eggplant halves. Sprinkle top with additional cracker crumbs. Bake one hour in a 350-degree oven, or until a silver knife inserted comes out clean. Serves four.*

## AMAZED AT GRACE

**FADE FROM A STILL PHOTOGRAPH OF A TODDLER ON HER GRANDFATHER'S KNEE** to video of a young woman stirring sauce.

"That's the third generation stirring," says Larry Proffitt in the kitchen of Ridgewood Barbecue. His daughter Lisa smiles, her image transformed from bonneted baby to business owner.

The knee she sits on in that photograph belongs to her late grandfather, Jim Proffitt, who made rayon during the week in Elizabethton, Tennessee, and blended barbecue sauce on the side in Bluff City. It's the sauce that University of North Carolina sociologist and native Tennessean Dr. John Shelton Reed would once describe as "what ketchup will taste like in heaven."

The ritualistic burning of the sauce recipe once a Proffitt family member has come of age and has earned the right to memorize it; the

**BUTTERMILK &
BIBLE BURGERS**

*Three generations of barbecue genius: Lisa Proffitt Peters, Larry Proffitt, and Grace Proffitt. Composite photo by Larry Smith.*

loyalty of employees like Brenda Fagan who have worked the tables at the Ridgewood for the majority of their adult lives; and the flat-out stubborn refusal of the restaurant's matriarch, Grace Proffitt, to let modernity force her into cutting corners: these were among the themes and stories that inspired my ETSU colleagues and me to create the film *Smoke in the Holler: The Saucy Story of Ridgewood Barbecue*.

Every fall I take my students on a field trip, a pilgrimage of sorts, to Bullock's Hollow in Sullivan County. On the way over, we talk about the beauty and the values of rural America. We pull into the graveled parking lot at the Ridgewood and walk down to the pit, with that day's hickory smoke still swirling around the building.

Then my students become part of a mini-course I like to call "The Wisdom and Philosophy of Larry Proffitt." He talks technique—the science of controlling the amount of air that enters the pit so that the fresh hams "smolder."

During these side-of-the-road lectures, he imparts the philosophy of his working-class parents.

"My mother used to say, 'People don't want to work for the man, for the woman. They want to work with the man, with the woman.'"

In 1987, a new four-lane highway was constructed just a mile and a half from the restaurant. Some predicted the closure of the Ridgewood. Grace took the change in stride. "We'll make it," her son remembers her saying. "We don't owe nothing."

Grace was right. "When they opened the new road, the business boomed," Larry tells the students.

Raised by two parents who knew the dignity of hard work, Larry Proffitt is one of the wisest people I know. He's an expert turkey hunter. A pharmacist. A farmer. He has a sophisticated education but has never forgotten the lessons of the fields, farmlands, and kitchens of Carter and Sullivan counties. He traverses a farm that has been in his family since 1856.

One of Larry Proffitt's lessons is persistence. Imagine a woman opening a beer joint in a secluded hollow in Sullivan County in 1948. Then imagine having the basis of the business wiped away a few years later when the county went dry. But Grace Proffitt refused to quit. As she says in the film, "I had two little boys to raise. I had to do something."

She and Jim borrowed the money to take those two little boys, Larry and Terry, on a vacation to Daytona Beach, Florida. There, the Proffitts came up with the idea of converting to barbecue, a decision that saved their business. And there, crossing Ridgewood Avenue a few blocks from the Atlantic Ocean, they discovered the name for their restaurant back in the hills of Tennessee.

Larry Proffitt remembers months when his mother never made a dime on the restaurant. Still, she kept on. Now, this third-generation business is testament to her determination.

Ridgewood Barbecue
900 Elizabethton Highway
Bluff City TN
423-538-7543

# BIG BOB: THE BARON OF NORTH ALABAMA BARBECUE

**BIG BOB GIBSON STANDS CONFIDENTLY AND PROUDLY,** looking off into the distance, with both hands on his hips. The year is 1956. In front of him and behind him, tables are stacked with plates of barbecue. Squares of store-bought light bread, three slices high, top every serving.

In the background, you can see the water tower for the city of Decatur, Alabama. Children of factory workers are seconds away from attacking Big Bob's handiwork, meat smoked over hickory wood. The occasion, Big Bob's descendants say, was likely a Monsanto company picnic.

*Big Bob Gibson caters a Monsanto company picnic in Decatur, Alabama, in 1956. Photo courtesy Chris Lilly.*

By the time that picture was taken, Big Bob had established a reputation as the baron of barbecue in northern Alabama. As a younger man, he had worked for the Louisville & Nashville railroad to keep food on the table for his wife, Ellen, known as Big Mama, and their six children. But his passion was barbecue, and he lived for the weekends when he could cook it in a hand-dug pit behind his house.

In 1925, he gave up railroading and took the risk of opening a restaurant. Big Bob Gibson's BBQ weathered the Depression that was to come four years later, and it still operates today, overseen by the same family—Big Bob's grandson, Don McLemore, and Chris Lilly, the husband of Big Bob's great-granddaughter.

Like Big Bob, Chris didn't start out his professional life as a barbecue pitmaster. With a marketing and finance degree from the University of North Alabama, he ended up in Franklin, Tennessee, selling scrub suits to health care companies.

"Either my father-in-law, Don McLemore, wanted to open up another restaurant in Decatur, or he wanted his daughter, my wife Amy, a little closer," Chris told me, in between national television appearances to promote his newest publication, *Big Bob Gibson's BBQ Book*. "I think it was the latter."

Building on the philosophies and techniques of Big Bob, Chris and Don have become international ambassadors for barbecue. "I have an offer right now to go to Denmark to hold a rib cooking class," says Chris, the reigning barbecue champion of Jamaica, where he cooked meat in fifty-five-gallon drums.

The Big Bob Gibson Bar-B-Q Competition Cooking Team has captured ten World BBQ championships, six world titles at Memphis in May, and the top spot in the American Royal International Cook-off and BBQ Sauce Competition in Kansas City.

"We never were satisfied with the red sauce we were serving on the tables of our restaurants," Chris says. "It was a commercial brand. So Don and I decided to make our own. We each tried to better the other's sauce, and we traded sauces for a year before he was satisfied and I was.

"We were going to the Memphis in May world championships, and we were both too stubborn to let the other one turn in their sauce. We mixed them together fifty-fifty and won the world championship. Don's wife, Carolyn, said, 'No more sauce-making. Bottle it as it is.'"

Chris describes it as "a cross between a Kansas City, a Memphis style, and a North Carolina sauce—tomato-based with a vinegar component."

As heralded and decorated as that red sauce has become, a white one, concocted by Big Bob himself in the 1920s, has trademarked his family's restaurants and influenced barbecue joints all across northern Alabama.

"Every chicken we cook, after it's done, we stick a fork in it and baptize it in barbecue white sauce," says Don in a film on Big Bob's produced by the Southern Foodways Alliance.

Chris says no one knows where Big Bob got the idea to stray so far from tomato-laced sauce, but customers soon started asking that bottles of his mayonnaise-vinegar-black pepper blend be placed on the restaurant's tables for pork shoulder.

Modern-day customers squirt it into barbecue-stuffed potatoes and use it as a salad dressing. Children bathe potato chips and soak bread with it.

"People ask if it tastes like ranch dressing, and that's not the case," Chris says. "Once I had a guy tell me he liked it on apple pie."

Chris has included the recipe in his book. It's a variation, he says, of the original, using mayonnaise, distilled white vinegar, apple juice, prepared horseradish, black pepper, fresh lemon juice, salt, and cayenne pepper. Big Bob's started bottling the sauce for commercial sale in 1997, and it's now distributed across the Southeast.

When Chris gave up medical sales to be a full-time barbecue man, he didn't want a desk job. Ledgers and balance sheets were secondary. Instead, he insisted on going in every day before six o'clock in the morning to work the pits.

"That's the barbecue business right there," he tells me. "It all starts in the pit room and how you smoke the meats."

Chris's book is a culmination of the hot, smoky experience, but more than that, it's a tribute to the six-foot, four-inch, 300-pound man who came to dominate the barbecue business on the banks of the Tennessee River.

"This is a story that had to be told," Chris says. "It's the story of Bob's life. He loved life, he loved people. Ever since I joined the family, this is something I've wanted to do—to celebrate Big Bob Gibson BBQ and Big Bob himself."

That old black-and-white picture of Big Bob at the company picnic opens Chris Lilly's book. "It's one of my favorite pictures," says Chris. "He's so proud of what he's done. That's the way he catered—paper plates, barbecue, and white bread."

*Big Bob Gibson Bar-B-Q*
*1715 6th Avenue, Southeast*
*Decatur AL*
*256-350-6969*

## Big Bob Gibson Bar-B-Q White Sauce

2 cups mayonnaise

1 cup distilled white vinegar

1/2 cup apple juice

2 teaspoons prepared horseradish

2 teaspoons ground black pepper

2 teaspoons fresh lemon juice

1 teaspoon salt

1/2 teaspoon cayenne pepper

*In a large bowl, combine all the ingredients and blend well. Use as a marinade, baste, or dipping sauce. Store refrigerated in an airtight container for up to 2 weeks. Makes 4 cups. (From Chris Lilly,* **Big Bob Gibson's BBQ Book: Recipes and Secrets from a Legendary Barbecue Joint***, 2009. Used with permission.)*

# FROM MADISONVILLE TO MANHATTAN
# WITH ALLAN BENTON

**ALLAN BENTON RARELY CARRIES A BUSINESS CARD.** He was a latecomer to the Internet. He never advertises. When David Chang, head of New York City's Momofuku restaurant group, requested information about Allan's products, what he got in return was a scroll of butcher paper with hand-written notes sketching the story of Benton's Smoky Mountain Country Hams in Madisonville, Tennessee.

Allan calls himself a "hillbilly," proudly, and labels his country ham and bacon store on Highway 411 a "hole-in-the-wall business."

He is a ham-curer and bacon-smoker of old. His techniques, and the many months they involve, have changed little from those of his grandparents, who were subsistence farmers in a secluded hollow in Scott County, Virginia.

*Allan Benton applies the cure. Photo by Larry Smith.*

Before Blackberry Farm in Walland, Tennessee, discovered him some twenty years ago, Allan says his "customer base consisted of a few locals and some greasy spoon restaurants." Now, this former high school guidance counselor is the talk of the pork world, and his goods span the continent.

"I couldn't have imagined, twenty years ago, that I would ever sell to one fine dining restaurant," Allan says. Now he estimates that his bacon and ham are served by around thirty restaurants in New York City alone, although it's still possible to walk into his Madisonville store and buy a roll of sausage or a slab of ham for the home kitchen.

"David Chang thinks nothing of ordering a couple hundred pounds of bacon ends or ham hocks at a time for the Momofuku restaurants, or just some ham bones and skins," says Allan. "He uses my products in ways that defy logic or gravity, as well as on charcuterie plates and in making stock to season mussels or clams."

Yet for Allan and his wife Sharon, the preferred cooking method for country ham is still the simple, ageless way they have appreciated since childhood: pan-frying in a black iron skillet.

*Benton's Smoky Mountain Country Hams*
*2603 Highway 411 North*
*Madisonville TN*
*423-442-5003*

## Allan Benton's Country Ham and Redeye Gravy

*Pour 1/4 cup of brewed coffee into an iron skillet and sprinkle in one tablespoon of brown sugar.*

*On medium heat, fry two or three slices of country ham for about two or three minutes per side. Remove ham and add 1/3 cup more coffee to the skillet.*

*Increase heat to medium-high and stir, loosening the browned particles from the bottom of the skillet.*

*Reduce the liquid to the point where you added the second measurement of coffee. Serve gravy over biscuits or grits.*

# THOMAS WOLFE'S "BIG EXTRAVAGANCE"

**"HEALTHIEST LOCATION/RATES REASONABLE"** reads the business card from 100 years ago.

As a boy, novelist Thomas Wolfe handed out such cards at the Asheville, North Carolina, train station, sent that way by his enterprising mother Julia, who ran the boardinghouse that would be called Dixieland in her son's 1929 book *Look Homeward, Angel.*

Julia Wolfe, who made business deals while her husband, W.O., ran a stone-carving shop on Pack Square, bought the Old Kentucky Home in

*Julia Wolfe ran this Asheville, North Carolina, boardinghouse while her son wrote novels. Photo by Fred Sauceman.*

1906 and began renting it out to boarders, many attracted to the community by the curative powers of the mountain air.

Actors preparing for the Vaudeville stage, shoe salesmen, patent medicine peddlers, temperance crusaders, and newlyweds took meals in Julia's dining room.

Remarkably, she provided a place to sleep and three meals for only one dollar a day. Boarders joked about how far she could stretch a coffee bean, complaining about coffee so weak you could see the bottom of the cup.

Wolfe often worried about the toll the business was taking on his mother. In a letter to her on June 3, 1927, he wrote, "I hope you have given up keeping boarders and roomers:—surely you have enough to keep you without going through that slavery again for third-rate people."

Tom was always known for his ravenous appetite, especially his capacity for biscuits, and some of the most memorable passages in *Look Homeward, Angel* describe the heavily laden tables at the boardinghouse.

"That is my big extravagance—my ravening gut," Tom wrote his mother on July 25, 1924, while teaching at New York University. "And when my mind has worked a few hours on books, papers, Creation—it calls for a different sort of food—meat, potatoes, pie."

Wolfe's mother often shipped him June apples and peaches from North Carolina, as well as oversized clothing to fit his 6'7" frame from Asheville's Bon Marché department store.

"I can truthfully say you could not have picked out any thing I needed more than socks, handkerchiefs, and ties," he told her in a letter sent from Brooklyn on October 12, 1931. "I was reduced to two pairs of unmatched socks with holes in the toes, and two neckties, each embroidered with the steak and gravy of the past three years."

Evoking strong memories of home for Wolfe, steak and gravy was a boardinghouse standard, and this version, reprinted in *Papa Loved Hot Biscuits and Corn Bread: Recipes from the Old Kentucky Home*, published in 1997 by the Thomas Wolfe Memorial Advisory Committee, was taken from a cookbook used by Julia Wolfe and her daughter Mabel Wolfe Wheaton.

 # Fried Steak

4    pieces of round steak, pounded (or cubed steak), about 20 ounces

1    cup flour

     Salt and pepper to taste

1    egg, lightly beaten

1 1/2 cups milk, divided

1/4  cup bacon grease, oil, or shortening

*Season flour with salt and pepper. Dredge meat in flour mixture.*

*Mix egg with one-half cup milk. Dip floured meat into milk mixture and then back into flour again.*

*Fry meat in large, heavy frying pan with bacon grease, oil, or shortening. Brown on both sides and remove from pan to drain on soft paper.*

*Keep warm on serving platter in oven.*

*Drain all remaining fat from pan except two tablespoons. Stir in two tablespoons flour mixture and scrape bottom of pan carefully to loosen drippings.*

*Using a whisk, stir in remaining milk and stir over medium heat until gravy thickens. If gravy becomes too thick, add more milk. Salt and pepper gravy to taste and serve over meat.*

# THE FIRST LADY OF RHUBARB

**THERE'S A DISCONNECT BETWEEN THE NAME OF THE RESTAURANT AND ITS OWNER.**
Louise Henson may be famous, but she doesn't show it.

Unassuming and humble, she runs Famous Louise's Rock House Restaurant near Linville Falls, just off the Blue Ridge Parkway in North Carolina. The river-rocked building was completed the year she was born, 1936.

The building is on the National Register, and Louise has been honored by the North Carolina House of Representatives.

She runs a restaurant known as much for its geography as its cuisine. Three North Carolina counties converge in the building.

The food is cooked in Avery County, picked up by the servers in Burke County, and consumed in Avery or McDowell. Louise tells me she pays her taxes in McDowell.

"I pay land tax in Avery," she adds. "Burke hasn't got me yet."

When she isn't bowling, Louise oversees the comings and goings at her restaurant from a special table, the only one covered with a red tablecloth.

Much of her "fame" is fed by rhubarb and her ability to balance its tartness with some sugar. She understands the yin and the yang of a strawberry-rhubarb pie.

She has been known to bake as many as forty of those pies in one day. The recipe she follows is her mother's. And, she says, her strawberry-rhubarb jam is just as popular as her pies among diners in Western North Carolina. It sits on a windowsill in her restaurant, its red hues catching the rays of the mountain sunshine.

"I was pulling rhubarb when I was twelve years old," says Louise, a native of Crossnore, North Carolina. "My grandparents, Pink and Madge Johnson, grew it. They would peddle it, take it Down East, around Durham and Winston-Salem, and sell it out of a pickup truck."

The fifty-seven-year veteran of the restaurant business buys much of her rhubarb locally. But sometimes she doesn't have to shell out a cent.

"Quite a few people give it to me," Louise says. "But a lot of people don't know what rhubarb is."

Lured off the Blue Ridge Parkway by the promise of true North Carolina country cooking, diners show up from all over the world. Laudatory comments about Louise's food, in many languages, fill several guest books.

At Famous Louise's Rock House Restaurant, every other Thursday is chicken and dumpling day. Louise's style of dumplings? Dropped and fluffy.

"People call me all the time wanting to know if it's dumpling week."

*"Famous Louise" is wild about rhubarb. Photo by Fred Sauceman.*

Famous Louise's
Rock House Restaurant
23175 Rockhouse Lane
(Linville Falls Highway)
Near Linville Falls NC
828-765-2702

# PERPETUATING GARDEN GOODNESS: THE CANNING OF BETTY ASCIONE

**BUTTERMILK & BIBLE BURGERS**

*Betty Ascione preserves the goodness of the garden by making chow-chow. Photo by Larry Smith.*

**THE WESTERN NORTH CAROLINA FARMERS MARKET** has been in operation for nearly forty years, at the confluence of Interstates 26 and 40 near Asheville. For most of that time, Betty Ascione has occupied a spot in the retail building, selling not only fresh garden produce and fruit but also her home canning.

"I have people come from all over the United States for my canning," says Betty. "I've always canned. I helped my mother out canning."

Betty married an Italian—hence her last name. But she's very much a Western North Carolina mountain lady, a Scroggs before marriage, from Leicester.

"If you live out there, it's pronounced LESTER," instructs Betty. "If you don't live out there, it's LEE-cester."

It was from her late mother, Pearl Scroggs, that she learned to can. The mountain relish called chow-chow that Betty sells so much of today is right out of her mother's kitchen.

"I put a lot more in my chow-chow than most people. My mother made it that way. I put green tomatoes in it, cucumbers, onions, red bell pepper, green bell pepper, and jalapeño pepper. Most people put it on soup beans, but it's good on hot dogs, good on hamburgers, and with tacos."

As soon as I got back home after my first visit with Betty, I followed her advice. I didn't cook up a pot of soup beans as a basis for chow-chow, as I normally would. Instead, I opted for hot dogs, those stark red Valleydale wieners. On the first one, I spread a thin coating of mustard on the bun, then scattered Betty's chow-chow across the dog. The chow-chow was so good, I decided the mustard just got in the way.

Nailed across the top of Betty's booth at the farmers market are framed blue ribbons she earned for her canning at the North Carolina Mountain State Fair near Arden. Her home kitchen is inspected regularly by the North Carolina Department of Agriculture, and she and her husband Ralph are graduates of the Better Process Control School at the University of Georgia. In short, Betty combines the best of the old, her mother's teaching, with the best of the new, the most modern sanitation techniques.

"Pickled beets, dilly beans, mixed pickles, green tomato pickles, bread and butter pickles, about any kind of pickle you want, I'll make," claims Betty proudly.

She says the hottest product in her repertoire is her hot jalapeño relish, a recipe she created using peppers out of her neighbor's garden.

"For good canning, you have to have fresh produce," says Betty. "The day you pick it, you put it in your jars, and that makes the best canning right there. If you let it sit two or three days, it won't be good. You get out of a jar what you put in it."

Western North Carolina
Farmers Market
Retail Building B
570 Brevard Road
Asheville NC
828-253-1691

BUTTERMILK &
BIBLE BURGERS

## THE SAVIOR OF A SENIOR CENTER

**THE CLINCHFIELD SENIOR ADULT CENTER GETS A LITTLE MONEY** from the town of Erwin, Tennessee, and the county of Unicoi, but not enough to keep the doors open and the exercise equipment tuned up, especially since members are charged only fifteen dollars a year to belong.

The savior of the senior center comes in a glass jar. Looking for a tie-in to the town's annual Apple Festival and a way to raise funds, executive director Charlene O'Dell remembered her grandmother Leona Ford serving apple relish in Cocke County, Tennessee. It's vinegar sour and hot pepper pungent, and Charlene likens it to salsa.

Members of the senior center work throughout the summer making the relish in the building's well-appointed, restaurant-quality kitchen.

BUTTERMILK &
BIBLE BURGERS

*Apple relish is highly valued in Unicoi County, Tennessee. Photo by Larry Smith.*

Charlene is a soft-spoken supervisor, but she's a stickler for consistency and food safety. As a young girl in Newport, she and a friend worked the green bean line at the Stokely-Van Camp cannery.

"Anything that got by us got in the can," she laughs.

Charlene insists that the cubes of Granny Smith apples that go into the relish measure half an inch and that all the pepper pieces be the same size.

Demand for apple relish now dictates the production of around 760 pints a year by an all-volunteer crew of cooks. In addition to apples and peppers, the simple, clear-cut recipe calls for onions, vinegar, and sugar.

Apple relish has transformed the kitchens of Unicoi County. Betty Peterson enlivens her potato salad with it. Linda Tolley rubs it on pork roasts. For an appetizer, party hosts drain the product and pour it over blocks of cream cheese. Apple relish adds an unconventional touch to traditional deviled eggs and chicken salad.

And for Charlene O'Dell, "Soup beans are not complete without apple relish."

The Clinchfield
Senior Adult Center
220 Union Street
Erwin TN
423-743-4521

**BUTTERMILK &
BIBLE BURGERS**

# THE BROCCOLI LADY

*Glodine Davis is known
all through East Tennessee
for her broccoli casserole.
Photo by Tony Duncan,
Johnson City Press.*

**ONE TASTE AND GLODINE DAVIS'S LIFE WAS TRANSFORMED.** She had grown up in
Covington, Tennessee, with a broccoli bias. She even married a man,
Ralph Davis, who shared her childhood distaste for the cruciferous vegetable. But after the first spoonful of her family's broccoli casserole, she
was a changed person.

"Oh, my goodness," she remembers saying. "I've got to have that recipe."

Dozens of people have said likewise over the years—so many, in fact, that Glodine now packs copies of her broccoli casserole recipe into her pocketbook anytime she brings the dish to a homecoming at Johnson City's Thankful Baptist Church, to a working lunch at Eastman Chemical Company in Kingsport, or to a meeting of the local NAACP chapter, such as the one I attended in December 2003, when I, too, fell under her casserole spell.

Glodine's broccoli casserole proffers a perfect combination: a green vegetable for the righteous, a whole stick of butter for the rowdy.

Broccoli casseroles in the South run a caloric gamut, with cream of mushroom soup the most common binding agent. In *Treasury of Tennessee Treats*, first published in 1957 by the Woman's Society of Christian Service at Keith Memorial Church in Athens, Tennessee, my aunt deviated by adding cream of celery and became downright revolutionary for her day by folding in water chestnuts. The recipe from Mrs. Joe T. Frye Jr., in that same book, calls for the complete pulverizing of the cooked broccoli with a potato masher, so that any hint of what we'd call dietary fiber today was forgotten.

In *The Memphis Cook Book*, published by that city's Junior League in 1964, Mrs. George S. Miles gussied up her recipe with separated eggs and called it a soufflé. *Main Street*, a 1980 cookbook from the Youth Builders in Greeneville, Tennessee, offers eleven different broccoli casserole variants, six of them bound with cream of mushroom soup. Three include Cheez Whiz, one Velveeta. Mary Helen McGruder submitted two versions, a soufflé and a "supreme," the latter containing a cup of sour cream.

Broccoli casserole creation, it seems, involves countless ways to balance the healthy properties of the vegetable with rich, indulgent dairy products.

But all those accoutrements never won over Ralph Davis. When he comes home and detects broccoli, he knows a covered dish dinner is in the offing somewhere.

Although Glodine remembers that first taste, she doesn't recall whether the recipe was handed down from an aunt in Covington or from her grandmother, Irene Murphy, who lived from 1900 to 1992. Either way, the casserole has traversed the three grand divisions of the state, from Covington in West Tennessee, to the student days of Glodine and Ralph at

Austin Peay State University in the Middle Tennessee city of Clarksville, and on to East Tennessee, where the Davises now make their home.

Enriched by that whole stick of butter, Glodine's broccoli casserole stays moist through repeated reheatings and remains flavorful and appetizing at room temperature. The topping is a common mid-twentieth-century touch: crushed, buttery crackers.

"It's almost a meal in itself, and you can mix it in the same bowl you bake it in," she tells me, as she knifes off squares of margarine for the casserole in her well-appointed Jonesborough kitchen, surrounded by a stack of recipes collected from family and friends over the years. She uses butter and margarine interchangeably in the broccoli casserole—whatever she has at hand, she explains.

To be so well known for a recipe is ironic for Glodine. Her grandmother Murphy never used recipes. When Glodine moved away from Covington, she called her grandmother often, seeking kitchen guidance—pleading that pinches and smidgeons be translated into fractions of teaspoons.

"She had barbecued or smothered chicken every Sunday for dinner," Glodine remembers. "She made the best blackberry cobbler and also a yellow cake she'd bake in an iron skillet. After the cake was done, you'd cut it up like you would cornbread, split it open, put butter in the middle, and pour a vanilla-flavored sauce, with the consistency of soft ice cream, over the top."

Irene Murphy called the cake "puddin'," and the family's love for it has been handed down to Ralph and Glodine's daughter Ralonda, along with a passion for her great-grandmother's meringue-topped chocolate pie.

"Everything my grandmother made, it seemed like it took all day," Glodine recalls. "She cooked everything very slowly. And we all ate supper together, at the same time."

The Davises are still divided over the taste of broccoli, but they're united in their amazement over the goodwill that Glodine's buttery, cheesy, West Tennessee broccoli casserole has created.

 ## Glodine Davis's Broccoli Casserole

2    boxes frozen chopped broccoli (Fred's note: I usually use fresh—two heads, cut into florets and boiled for about five minutes.)

2    cans cream of mushroom soup

1    small onion, chopped

1    stick butter or margarine, cut into thin slices

2    eggs, beaten

1½ cups grated cheddar cheese

    Crushed Ritz or Town House crackers for topping

*Cook and drain broccoli.*

*Add remaining ingredients and mix well.*

*Sprinkle crushed cracker crumbs on top and bake at 350 degrees for about an hour, until bubbly.*

## ELOISE

*Eloise Swain tells stories
with her Hawaiian hands.
Photo by Fred Sauceman.*

**ON TUESDAY MORNINGS AT NINE O'CLOCK SHARP, ELOISE SWAIN WOULD TEE OFF** at Pine Oaks Golf Course in Johnson City, Tennessee. Friday nights she presided over karaoke at her family's neighborhood bar, The Cottage. Eloise turned eighty-five years old on September 16, 2011.

Her long and active life has ranged from the sugar plantations of her native Hawaii to the bingo halls of Southwest Virginia. Whether answering the telephone at the Bank of Hawaii or learning to fry milk-soaked chicken and hefty cheeseburgers in The Cottage's kitchen, she has always worn a flower in her hair. It's part of her go-to-work attire and a remembrance of life on the islands.

Most Friday nights at The Cottage, you'd find her in a muumuu. She has a closet full. And on one particular Friday night every year, a muumuu was mandatory. It was the Friday in June that fell closest to the birthday of King Kamehameha, who united the Hawaiian Islands. The Cottage karaoke party ramped up that night, often spilling out into the parking lot.

The party reminded Eloise of her days as a schoolgirl back on the "big island" of Hawaii, when hula competitions were held in the schools in memory of the king, "the Napoleon of the Pacific," who died in 1819.

*Eloise (left) and her sister Lehua, early 1940s. Photo courtesy Eloise Swain.*

All the old dance moves came back to her on this special Friday night—the flowing arms, the graceful fingers, the gently swaying hips, all telling a story.

Amid the raucousness of beer-fueled karaoke, when Eloise stepped out from behind the bar and Theresa Greer cued up "Lovely Hula Hands," The Cottage crowd got totally quiet. For three minutes, Eloise, smiling broadly and lithe as a teenager, was the center of attention.

With pineapples as door prizes and leis around every neck, for one night, this bar in the uplands of East Tennessee turned tropical. Although the owners of The Cottage love the mountains and, as Eloise says, love "being able to drive from one state to another," Hawaii is never far from their minds. Eloise's sister, the late Ellenmerle Heiges, owned the bar for many years with her husband, Don. When Ellenmerle died in late 2010, the family requested that visitors to the funeral home wear Hawaiian shirts, and the funeral parlor was a festival of flowers.

Eloise's first job in Hawaii was driving a tractor between rows of sugar cane at the Hutchinson Sugar Plantation, where her father, Louis, supervised the tractor drivers and her mother, Rose, made clothes. During World War II, schools were closed on Fridays so students could work in the cane fields.

Eloise later took a job in wholesale retail, then went to work as a switchboard operator for the Bank of Hawaii. On a dare, she accepted a job at the Seven Seas restaurant in Hilo. That led to a position as a bar manager at a place in Hilo she describes as "like The Cottage but with pool tables and liquor."

In 1981, after a divorce, Eloise left Hawaii for the mainland, and thus began her love affair with the mountains of East Tennessee and her ongoing love affair with customers at The Cottage. Along the way, her family came to include two children, five grandchildren, and three great-grandchildren.

Holidays at the Heiges house are celebrated around a black iron skillet full of Eloise's fried rice, a dish treasured by her niece and nephew, Patti and Sonny Heiges, who inherited The Cottage from their parents. Her teriyaki chicken and kimchee are legendary around Johnson City, too.

The family tree of Eloise Swain is populated by a number of soldiers. Her oldest brother, Wesley Swain, was wounded in the Philippines during World War II and died on the operating table. Her brother Benjamin went missing in action during the Korean War and was never found. Her brother-in-law, Don, spent thirty years as a Marine Corps staff sergeant before taking ownership of The Cottage. He had staffed an NCO Club in Okinawa and met his future wife, Ellenmerle, a nurse, at a USO party in Hawaii. Opening a place like The Cottage was Don's dream.

Just as her brother-in-law did, Eloise immediately associates a face with a beer brand. Customers rarely had to say a word on Friday nights, as their Budweisers and Millers were served up before elbows touched the bar.

It takes a good memory to tend bar. Eloise says it takes patience, too. She tolerated all gradations of karaoke ability and decibel levels with her ever-present smile.

Around her neck, Eloise wears a dark necklace. It's made of kukui nuts. The symbolism is fitting. Oil from the nuts was used for lamplight on the Hawaiian Islands. Kukui, Eloise explains, means "light." It's something she brings into the lives of her family and friends every day.

Note: In the summer of 2012, Eloise, after great sadness on her last night of karaoke in Tennessee, returned home to her native Hilo, Hawaii, where she continues to play golf with a flower in her hair.

The Cottage
705 West Market Street
Johnson City TN
423-928-9753

# RAVIOLI AND RECOVERY:
# THE SPIRIT OF LOBELLO'S SPAGHETTI HOUSE

**ROSE LOBELLO HAS STIRRED DOWN RED SAUCE FOR NEARLY SEVENTY YEARS.** She's never traveled to Italy, the land of her ancestors. She couldn't abandon her family's restaurant for that long.

Except for a few weeks when the place sold "West Virginia hot dogs," LoBello's Spaghetti House has plated up Italian-American fare in Coraopolis, Pennsylvania, northwest of Pittsburgh, since 1944.

Rose started working in her parents' restaurant that year, when she was fourteen. Spaghetti, gnocchi, and ravioli took over her life. Kitchen labor kept her from graduating high school.

*LoBello's serves up classic Italian-American goodness near Pittsburgh, Pennsylvania. Photo by Fred Sauceman.*

*Rose LoBello stirred pasta sauce for years in the back of the house. Now she's the perfect hostess out front. Photo by Fred Sauceman.*

"My mother never really had a childhood," says her daughter, Rosalie Richards, of Moon Township, Pennsylvania.

Rose later raised her own children in the restaurant. They napped in lettuce crates while she hand-mixed pasta dough. She cut gnocchi strips and hand-cranked them through a machine. She managed cauldrons of sauce and blended house-made salad dressing. She mixed and formed her own meatballs. She reveled in coconut cream and banana cream pies. She waited tables. She ran the cash register.

Since 2005, though, Rose has left the heavy lifting and the arm-tiring pasta making to her son Ben. After her foot was crushed in an automobile accident, Rose began taking large doses of Aspirin. A blood vessel ruptured in her brain. She survived the surgery to undergo months of extensive therapy, both physical and occupational.

"One of my three brothers, John, is a songwriter," says Rosalie. "He is very methodical, and his approach helped get her through."

Her therapists understood, too, that Rose LoBello's life had revolved around food, and they slowly reintroduced her to the kitchen.

"I made gnocchi for the nurses," Rose told my wife and me, after a meal of lasagna and ravioli in her restaurant.

"That's how they started to rehabilitate her, by taking her into the kitchen, because the health care professionals thought they should give her something to do that she was good at," recalls Rosalie.

Although she's forbidden to lift a pot of sauce today because of her health, she can still season one, adding salt four times in a circle.

"My mother recovered remarkably," says Rosalie. "She never was a big talker, and that's the biggest change in her since the surgery. She's much more talkative."

Just as she's done with so many of the hardships in her life, Rose has turned a near-death experience into something good. That newfound verbosity has transformed her into the perfect hostess at LoBello's.

As her son Ben boils ravioli and fills manicotti in the kitchen, Rose moves to the front of the house, gliding from table to table, greeting customers as if she's known them her entire lifetime. She stopped by our table

_LoBello's Spaghetti House_
_809 5th Avenue_
_Coraopolis PA_
_412-264-9721_

repeatedly, each time adding a chapter from her life story—talk of her father's work in the coal mines, her love of dancing, her Italian heritage, how she married her husband without ever having a date.

"Everyone knows her," says Rosalie.

"We were at McDonald's having coffee, as we do from time to time just to get her out, and a little girl, maybe eight years old, comes up and gives her a hug. My mother calls kids her 'little angels.'"

Over a cup of homemade Italian wedding soup, the diminutive Rose LoBello shared with us her philosophy of life, in four short words: "I just love people."

# GETTING LESSONS IN BETWEEN

**BESSE BROWN'S AZURE EYES BRIGHTENED** when her parents told her a new school was being built only nine miles from her home in Boones Creek, Tennessee. She had always wanted to be a teacher, ever since first grade.

*Besse Brown during her college years at East Tennessee State Normal School. Photo courtesy the Sidney Cooper family.*

That new school opened on October 2, 1911, in Johnson City, a post-Civil War railroad community. In fact, it was a railroad man, George L. Carter, who made sure Johnson City would win the town-against-town battle and be the home of East Tennessee State Normal School. Multimillionaire Carter, whose laborers had laid out the Clinchfield Railroad and whose coal mines fueled its locomotives, gave away his farm so Besse Brown and others with similar ambitions could study practical subjects like running a household, alongside theoretical ones like Latin poetry.

Above all, East Tennessee State Normal School was created to educate competent and polished teachers. In Besse Brown's day, there were people teaching in the public schools who had no college training at all. Some hadn't even finished high school. And so, in an effort to raise the level of literacy and knowledge all across the state, the Tennessee General Assembly passed a bill in 1909 calling for the creation of normal schools in each of the three grand divisions, East, Middle, and West.

That legislation would change Besse Brown's life. She hopped a train in Gray Station and rode to Johnson City, where she boarded with an aunt. From there she rode a trolley car to the site of Carter's former farm, now populated with professors who held higher education pedigrees from all over the world.

She took her education seriously. To chemistry class one day in 1914, she wore her very best dress. But a chemical solution spilled out of an errant test tube and ruined it. She never forgot the incident.

Besse Brown Cooper wore her Normal School class ring for ninety-two years. It had to be cut off her finger in October of 2009.

"Her hand was swelling, and the staff at the nursing home feared that the ring might cut off my mother's circulation, so they asked permission to cut off the ring," says her son Sidney. "That ring was worn completely slick, as smooth as this tabletop. She never took it off. She wore it when she gardened, washed clothes, when she cooked."

Sidney Cooper himself is a symbol of his mother's fondness for the Normal School and the opportunities it gave her. Her third of four children, he is named for the very first president of East Tennessee State Normal School, Sidney G. Gilbreath, a man Besse Cooper deeply admired.

Other than that discarded dress, Besse's only disappointment about her education at the Normal School was the dropping of German classes. Caught in the xenophobia that swept the country when World War I broke out in 1914, administrators at the Johnson City school cut German from the curriculum.

"Mother loved every subject she ever studied," said her son. "At that period of time, a country girl going to college was pretty rare.

"That education stayed with her. She read constantly. She encouraged us to read. We got books for Christmas. She read the comics to us every Sunday."

Besse Cooper became the world's oldest person on January 31, 2011, upon the death of Eunice G. Sanborn of Jacksonville, Texas. Besse's grandson Paul, who visited her almost every day, was the first to break the news.

"When she became the oldest person in the world, I had the good fortune to tell her," said Paul. "She paused and said, 'No, honey, I don't think so.' 'Yes, ma'am,' I said, 'the woman in Texas passed away this morning, and you're the oldest person in the world. How does that feel?'

"She paused and she said, 'Well, I think it feels pretty good.' And then she paused again and said, 'I think I'd like a box of chocolates.'

"I said, 'Which kind would you like?'

"'I'd like the assorted kind,' she answered."

When Paul brought the box of chocolates into his grandmother's room, he told her he was going to read aloud the names of the candy varieties and asked her to stop him when he came to just the right one for her first taste. He read off raspberry, dark chocolate, truffle. And then coconut. That's when his grandmother stopped him.

"Oh, you used to make the best coconut cake," Paul remembered.

"I know I did, didn't I?" she answered.

"And then she looked at me and said, 'I still do.'"

Paul visited his grandmother usually at night, and they conversed for about thirty minutes. Often their talk turned to food: collard greens versus turnips. Biscuits. Apple pie. Sauerkraut. Foods Besse had been loyal to ever since she lived in Tennessee.

"Cooking was always conveyed to me by her as a joy, not a burden, not something she became tired of," Paul tells me. "She spoke of food in a very fond, passionate way. Her biscuits were absolutely the best. They weren't too doughy and not too hard. They weren't too lard-laden or fried-tasting."

"She could make anything out of apples," Sidney adds. "Butter, jelly, sauce. She grew apples in Tennessee and could make the best apple pie. Here in Georgia she would go out and pick up these gnarled apples, ones I wouldn't even bother with. A few days later she'd have a nice apple pie made out of them.

"She didn't let anything go to waste. She knew what to do on a farm. She grew winter squash here in Georgia when nobody around had heard of it. She knew how to cure meat, smoke sausage."

Sidney said his mother was always interested in politics. When women were given the right to vote in 1920, she was among the first to register them in Walton County, Georgia.

She voted in the 2008 presidential election, and when she learned that an African American man had won, she told her grandson, "I think that's a very good thing."

It was the promise of better money at the end of World War I that led Besse from the schoolhouse in Tiger Valley, Tennessee, to a place called Between, equidistant from Loganville and Monroe, Georgia, on Highway 78, the main route to Atlanta before the coming of the interstates.

In Between, she took over a two-room school that, Sidney said, she "straightened out." Another teacher was responsible for the first three grades, and Besse taught grades four through seven. When she learned that some unruly students upset a previous teacher so badly she had to go out and walk the sidewalk to regain her composure, Besse reportedly said, "If anybody walks up and down the sidewalk it'll be them. It won't be me."

The school in Between would eventually be rated the best in the county.

Sidney said his mother was always in control, in charge. When he started attending the little school in Between in 1941, he was one of the last students in the springtime to cast off his shoes.

"Here everyone else was barefoot, and I was ordered to keep wearing shoes until very late in the spring by my mother," Sidney recalled. He jokingly told her that sometimes he wished he had a Georgia mother, since Tennessee mothers were too strict.

By the time Sidney entered school, his mother had given up teaching, but she insisted on checking her four children's homework, and Sidney said she was especially skillful in talking him through word problems. "She taught me to like mathematics," he added.

Sidney would go on to be an industrial engineer in the apparel industry.

Besse never lived in Tennessee again after departing for Georgia in 1918, but she and her family would come back to Boones Creek about once a year and spend a week in what they called the "home house."

"We love the lush, green countryside and pasture fields of East Tennessee," Sidney said.

One of Sidney's favorite stories, though, involves his grandparents' aborted attempt to leave the state, in November 1900, for Arkansas, the "land of opportunity." Besse's parents and uncle and aunt built a houseboat and got as far downriver as Chattanooga, where they were grounded on a sandbar in the middle of the Tennessee. They were advised to return to Upper East Tennessee because of a yellow fever outbreak in Arkansas, and they built the two-story "home house" on fifteen acres of land in Boones Creek. Besse remembered that river trip because at age four she was tied around the waist with rope to keep her from tumbling into the cold waters of November.

Sidney and Paul talk lovingly and at length about the astonishing life of Besse Cooper. Among their most vivid memories is hearing her singing in the kitchen: "Life Is Like a Mountain Railroad," a song that reminded her of riding the narrow-gauge tracks on the way to her first teaching job in Carter County, Tennessee.

Sidney laughs when he thinks of how his mother impressed her cousins by subscribing to the *Ladies' Home Journal* in the 1930s. He marvels at the fact that his mother never had surgery.

Besse lived on her own until she was 105. Once she reached the age of 110, staff from the *Guinness Book of World Records* initiated regular contact with her family.

Among the red-letter days of my life was February 22, 2011, when I had the opportunity to be in the presence of Besse Cooper, less than a month after she became the world's oldest person. She had her hair done that day, in preparation for our visit, and she put her teeth in, a sign, her family says, that something good was anticipated that day.

I avoided the obvious "secret to a long life" question, knowing it would arise naturally in my conversations with Sidney and Paul.

"My grandmother never worried about the things she couldn't affect," says Paul. "She was not a worrier. Everything was interesting to her, and everything was something to learn. She enjoyed watching her grandchildren make the world a better place.

"It's very humbling, knowing so many people much younger are suffering and in poor health. To have lived a life this long and of this quality is just phenomenal. She has enriched my life in ways I can't even describe to you."

Besse Cooper died on December 4, 2012, at age 116 years and 100 days. She is buried in Between.

 ## Besse Cooper's Swiss Steak

1   pound round steak, cut into serving pieces

    Salt and pepper

    Flour

3   tablespoons Crisco

1   onion, sliced

4   ripe tomatoes, skinned and chopped

*Pound the steak. Salt and pepper it and dip in flour.*

*Have the Crisco melted and hot in a Dutch oven. Brown the steak on both sides. Cover with water. Add onions and tomatoes.*

*Cover and simmer for 3 hours. When done the gravy is already made and is delicious.*

 # Besse Cooper's Boiled Custard

4   cups sweet milk

1/2   cup sugar or more if you like it sweeter

1/4   teaspoon salt

2   whole eggs

3   egg yolks

1   teaspoon vanilla

*Mix the milk, sugar, and salt and scald in a double boiler.*

*Beat the eggs thoroughly. Stir some of the hot milk into the eggs. Put the egg mixture into the boiler with the milk and vanilla and cook until it coats a spoon.*

*Stir all the time while it is cooking. Strain it.*

*If it cooks too long, it will not be smooth. Beat it with a mixer on high.*

*Pour into a serving bowl and chill.*

## ROSY SERVES UP SASS

**IT'S ONE OF THE MOST IDENTIFIABLE LANDMARKS IN KNOXVILLE, TENNESSEE.** Right up there with the Sunsphere, Neyland Stadium, and the tower of Ayres Hall at the University of Tennessee. It's constructed not of steel and bricks but rather of ink and white space. Rosy's Diner is a Knoxville symbol, and its saucy, red-headed proprietor is one of the city's most recognizable personalities.

Rosy and her diner are the creations of *Knoxville News Sentinel* editorial cartoonist Charlie Daniel, who has been chronicling life in his adopted city since 1958.

BUTTERMILK &
BIBLE BURGERS

*Rosy's is East Tennessee's
most popular imaginary
diner. Cartoon courtesy the
legendary Charlie Daniel.*

Charlie may be the artist, the conduit, but there's no question who's in charge at Rosy's. Prominently posted on the wall is one of her firm rules: No Hat, No Service.

Rosy's sole exception to the "No Hat, No Service" dictum occurs on November 11, when she posts a sign reading "Hats Off to Our Veterans" and features a Hero Sandwich as the daily special.

Always attuned to current events, Rosy often serves up a topical menu. When oil spewed into the Gulf of Mexico, one of her regulars, who always sports a UT ballcap, asked her what kind of shrimp she had.

"Popcorn, jumbo, and 10W40," she shot back.

A University of North Carolina graduate, Charlie manages to sneak some light blue into his cartoons. C. D. Smidlap, a longtime Rosy's patron, often shows up in a Carolina blue shirt. But Rosy is a loyal Volunteer, from the color of her hair to the hue of her gravy.

"Rosy guards her secrets like Colonel Sanders," says Charlie, "but I do suspect that orange food coloring may be involved in her Vol Navy Gravy."

Odd-colored gravy and all, Rosy is proud of what she plates up. One Thanksgiving, a customer called her the "Michelangelo of Meatloaf Molding."

Growing up (a term he uses loosely) in Weldon, North Carolina, Charlie had no intention of becoming an editorial cartoonist, or a cartoonist of any sort. But then he started doodling, and people noticed.

"I was going to be a football player and a football coach," he tells me. "I went to Fork Union Military Academy, and I discovered, about 1949, a copy of Bill Mauldin's *Up Front*. I fell in love with his drawings.

"Through Bill Mauldin I learned to have a healthy disrespect for authority. I still had no idea of becoming a cartoonist. I'd gone into the Marines, and I came back and was in business school at the University of North Carolina, and a friend of mine noticed all these doodles that I kept doing, and he said, 'You're a cartoonist,' which came as news to me. He drug me kicking and screaming down to *The Daily Tar Heel* to submit some drawings, and they said they would run them and they would take me on as their political cartoonist, and so that's how I got started. I switched from business to political science because once I saw one published, I was hooked."

Looking back over a sixty-year career in cartooning in Knoxville, Charlie appreciates the freedom his publishers have given him every day to

create his own world—a world where an orange blue-tick coonhound ter-
rorizes a purple and yellow LSU Tiger. Where the Easter Bunny
announces to a group of children that he's putting their Easter eggs in personal retirement accounts. And where people don't take much stock in
salads. Thin people don't eat at Rosy's Diner. Gaunt is out of fashion there.
Fleshy is in. Rosyburgers and Rosyfries, hefty and caloric, are the order of
the day, along with a dose of counter stool spunkiness from Rosy, created
by a man who says his greatest reward is having his work stuck on the
refrigerator.

# PART TWO
# THE PRODUCTS

# AN INVESTMENT IN IRON

**JERRY DON AND CAROL KING OWN ABOUT A DOZEN CAST-IRON SKILLETS.** In their home, in the Sweden's Cove section of Marion County, Tennessee, skillets sit on the bar all the time, for decoration. More than that, though, they symbolize family tradition.

Jerry Don is one of 220 employees who make cast-iron skillets and an array of accompanying products at Lodge Manufacturing in South Pittsburg, Tennessee. Jerry Don's grandfather, John King, started working at Lodge in the 1930s. Jerry Don's father, Albert, also worked there. Three of Jerry Don's uncles worked there. Jerry Don's brother worked there.

Lodge itself is a family business, now in the hands of the fourth generation of Lodges and Kellermanns. Dating to 1896, it is the oldest family-owned cookware company in America.

**BUTTERMILK & BIBLE BURGERS**

*Located in South Pittsburg, Tennessee, Lodge Manufacturing is the oldest family-owned cookware company in America. Photo by Fred Sauceman.*

Jerry Don King took a job at Lodge immediately after graduating from South Pittsburg High School, and he has spent his entire working life with the company, nearly forty years. His title now is Utility Mechanic, meaning he has to know virtually every phase of the complex operation. He started out in the packing room, putting labels on skillets.

Jerry Don says the company owners told him that if he planned to stay on at Lodge, he should learn about everything in the plant, a little at a time. He took the advice.

"I picked up welding when I got a chance," he says. "The same with the cutting torch. I've gone from packing to finishing to the foundry."

Working at Lodge means constant learning. While the iconic cast-iron skillet remains the centerpiece of the business, the product line has expanded to some 120 items. About thirty years ago, for example, Lodge started making woks. Seasoned steel pans and skillets were recently added. The fifteen-inch seasoned skillet resembles a Spanish paella pan. Within the last few years, grill pans have become quite popular. "People like grill marks on their food," says Mark Kelly, PR and Advertising Manager for Lodge.

A former newspaper and magazine editor, Mark has been a fan of cast iron all his life. His grandparents' Dutch oven, given to them as a wedding present in 1918, is still in use. (It's not the only relic Mark inherited from them, by the way. As a mortician's apprentice, Mark's grandfather, Robert Hoge, was one of the people who embalmed William Jennings Bryan after the Scopes Trial in Dayton, Tennessee. Mark says the rear handle of Bryan's casket fell off, and his grandfather kept it. Mark, who appreciates a good Southern gothic story, keeps the handle in a drawer at home.)

Lodge Manufacturing was started by an Englishman, Joseph Lodge, who walked from Chattanooga to South Pittsburg, some thirty miles, in search of a place to locate a foundry.

"Joseph Lodge always said there are a thousand ways to make cast iron wrong and only one way to do it right," says Mark, who describes what takes place in the foundry as "Middle Ages technology," automated. From

BUTTERMILK &
BIBLE BURGERS

the pouring of the molten metal to the packing of the product, the entire process now takes about ninety minutes, and the foundry's capacity ranges from 800 to 1,600 pieces per hour.

As in most every industry, the making of cast iron has its own language. Buckets are bulls. Each pour of molten metal is a charge. A key to the whole process, though, is simply sand. "It's ancient technology," Mark says.

Sand can withstand the intense heat of the liquid iron, which is poured into molds at temperatures between 2,480 and 2,520 degrees. Vibrating, cleaning, tumbling, and blasting with fine steel shot remove any excess sand. The sand itself and the steel shot are all recycled. Scrap steel and cast iron are recycled as well.

"We recycle virtually everything," Mark says. "Foundries have always been sustainable. We use that sand over and over, and then it goes to line landfills, ponds, and into mortar for bricks."

In 2011, Lodge recycled seventy-eight tons of cardboard, 399 tons of metal scrap, and 960 gallons of seasoning oil. The company started seasoning its products in 2002, and by 2007, all Lodge products were leaving the foundry in seasoned form.

Mark Kelly compares the seasoning to what goes on in a car wash. Vegetable oil is sprayed onto both sides of the products with electrostatic spray guns. The chemistry is simple: The positively charged oil atoms bond with the negatively charged iron atoms. The familiar black patina results when the products are then baked in a high-temperature oven.

Each generation, it seems, is rediscovering the benefits of cast-iron cookware, which only gets better with age. "Doctors say if you have anemia, cook with cast iron," says Mark. "It's such a simple thing."

Demand for ten-inch and twelve-inch skillets increases annually.

"Every year, Amazon does projections on sales at the holidays. During the 2012 holiday season, Lodge represented five of the top ten-selling cookware items," says Mark. Some 3,000 dealers carry Lodge products, and that's counting Wal-Mart as one dealer. "High-end" stores like Sur la Table and Williams-Sonoma now do a brisk business in Lodge's American-made cast iron.

Lodge runs several outlet stores, including one adjacent to the foundry. It's a favorite stop for visitors to the National Cornbread Festival, held in downtown South Pittsburg every April. Lodge and Martha White Flour are the original sponsors of the event.

"The downtown area was dying," says Mark. "The bypass took the traffic away. The festival was a way to reinvigorate the city."

While cast-iron cookware is evolving, with additions such as enamel coating in various colors, Lodge has achieved a perfect balance between keeping up with trends in technology and tastes and yet staying true to the old methods.

"We make a number-one quality product," says Jerry Don King. "That's what has gotten people's attention over the years. When you buy cast-iron cookware, you're buying a partner for life, something you can pass down to your children. It's one of the smartest investments a person can make."

## Tomato Gravy

Drippings from 2 cooked bacon slices

2  large ripe tomatoes, finely chopped

1  large Vidalia onion, chopped

Dash of Tabasco sauce

1/2  teaspoon salt

1/4  teaspoon freshly ground black pepper

1/4  cup all-purpose flour

1  cup leftover coffee

*Heat bacon drippings in a well-seasoned 12-inch cast-iron skillet over medium-high heat. Add the tomatoes and onion, stirring until the onion is softened, about 5 minutes.*

*Add the Tabasco, salt, and pepper. Add the flour and cook, stirring constantly, until the mixture thickens.*

*Gradually add the coffee and bring the mixture to a boil, stirring constantly. Reduce the heat to medium-low and cook until thickened, about 5 minutes, stirring constantly. Serve over biscuits.*

*Reprinted with permission from The Lodge Cast Iron Cookbook: A Treasury of Timeless, Delicious Recipes. ©2012, Lodge Manufacturing Company.*

## BEATING BISCUITS

**THE ADJECTIVES MOST COMMONLY APPLIED TO BISCUITS TODAY ARE "FLUFFY" AND "LIGHT."**
But "filling" and "long-lasting" were once the criteria for a good biscuit.

Fluffy biscuits are fairly modern creations, a result of the widespread availability of leavening agents. Commercial baking soda became available around 1840. Baking powder was introduced in 1856. And commercial yeast first went on the market in the United States in 1868.

The doubly light, extra fluffy angel biscuits described in church circle cookbooks are quite new, with both yeast and baking powder leavening the flour. Buttermilk produces just the right chemical reaction and adds enough moisture to create that treasured lightness.

*Kentucky beaten biscuits cradle country ham. Photo by Larry Smith.*

Two centuries ago, however, long before mechanization and chemistry took over, biscuit making involved vigorous labor—clubbing dough until arms throbbed. The result was the beaten biscuit, with a shelf life of about a month.

To make a beaten biscuit, the dough of flour, lard, and milk was whacked variously with mallets, skillets, axes, or even baseball bats. The continuous folding and flattening of the dough made it soft and smooth. The layering and pounding introduced air and made the biscuits rise a bit in the oven.

In the late nineteenth century, J. A. DeMuth of St. Joseph, Missouri, lightened the labor by manufacturing what came to be known as a biscuit brake, a machine with two nickel-plated rollers mounted on a marble slab, supported by a cast-iron base like that of a sewing machine.

It saved the beaten biscuit, and it's exactly the kind of apparatus used today by John and Judy Jackson in Winchester, Kentucky. For well over thirty years, the Jacksons have been cranking out beaten biscuits, now in their garage. They prick nine holes in every biscuit as entry points for heat to help the biscuits rise ever so slightly. In a year's time, the Jacksons turn out around 5,000 beaten biscuits.

Most of them envelop country ham. Kentucky, in the heart of the country ham belt, is, without doubt, the beaten biscuit capital of the world.

While we extol and enjoy fluffy biscuits, it's important not to forget the much longer history of the beaten variety and the axes, baseball bats, and hand-cranked machinery that have been laboriously employed to bring them to the tables of the South.

## BREAKING BEANS

*Old Walker Sister Beans from the Great Smoky Mountains in Tennessee, grown for generations by the Hatcher and Ogle families. Photo by Fred Sauceman.*

**KENTUCKY WONDERS. HALF-RUNNERS. TURKEY CRAWS. GREASY CUT-SHORTS.** Just the terms themselves conjure summertime memories. Green beans are among the land's most precious gifts this time of year.

If you've ever broken a bean, you'll never forget the snap and then the ping you hear when you toss it into an enamel pan. Green bean snap and ping are two of summer's most unforgettable sounds.

I've heard my people talk of breaking beans all my life. My parents broke them, they tell me, the day before I was born. The breaking always brought forth speculation on how weather affected the thickness of the bean strings and talk of long-forgotten varieties like the Myers Family

Bean of Greene County, Tennessee. Never trust a stringless bean, I was always told.

There's a rhythm to the breaking of beans. And a ritual—of fan-swept front porches, antique pans, scallop-shaped metal chairs, and newspapers in laps.

In the 1930s, when my grandmother heard the engine of the produce truck echoing off the pavement of Carson Street in Greeneville, Tennessee, she'd grab a pan and head to the house of the buyer to offer her services as volunteer bean-breaker, no compensation or trade for labor required.

Green beans brought out the best in folks. They still do. My father always said the more green beans you gave away, the better your plants produced.

My friend Bill Best, a North Carolinian who now lives in Berea, Kentucky, knows more about green beans than anyone I've ever met. Bill's a seed-saver, preserving what we've come to call heirloom varieties. He told me once about a Noble Bean, probably named for a family but also, I'd like to think, for its character.

This bean once traveled from West Virginia to Oregon. The great-granddaughter of the man who brought the bean to the Northwest sent Bill some seeds that weren't germinating. They'd been in a container for about twenty years. Meticulously, Bill coaxed six seeds out of one hundred to germinate. All of them died but one. From that one plant, he saved eleven seeds.

"If I'm lucky," he says, "I will have helped bring this bean back from extinction."

Green beans are as resilient as the mountain people who cherish them. Archaeologists tell us that green beans have been growing in the Appalachians for at least 1,400 years.

"These were cut-short varieties, with beans so closely packed that they square off on the ends," Bill says. "Cut-shorts would have been highly valued by native peoples because of their high protein content. They're still highly valued today."

So are Greasy Beans. In fact, Bill Davidson, owner of Davidson's Country Store and Farm near Rogersville, Tennessee, calls them "the green bean connoisseur's green bean." And they're named not for taste and texture but rather for their slick, oily-looking appearance. As green beans go, they're finicky. If the temperature reaches seventy degrees at night and stays there for a while, they can abort their blooms.

No matter the variety, in the kitchen, green beans adapt well to the speed of the pressure cooker or the languor of the Dutch oven, to the opulence of fatback or the prudence of olive oil.

They freeze, they can, they pickle. And for those unbroken, they dry and rattle, threaded onto a piece of string as "leather britches," their richness to be reconstituted in water long after the growing season has ended.

"Beans were woven into the fabric of everything we did as a family and community," remembers Bill Best.

Those backyard, under-the-maple-trees bean-breaking sessions attracted neighbors, grandparents, and cousins, brought together by the immediate promise of green beans and new potatoes right off the stove, as well as the hope of a warm weather meal and memory come winter.

# RED-EYE GRAVY REINTERPRETED

**IT MAY BE THE WORLD'S SIMPLEST GRAVY.** The most elemental version involves two ingredients and no tricky thickening.

Water and what's left in a black-iron skillet after country ham is fried are all it takes to make red-eye gravy. No salt, no seasoning, no herbs. Just leavings and liquid. And maybe a little leftover coffee. Writer and food historian John Egerton calls red-eye gravy a "divine elixir."

Researching red-eye yields some questionable stories about the name of the dish. Andrew Jackson's alleged observation about the red eyes of a hung-over cook is among them.

As with much of our food history, though, we'll probably never know who named red-eye gravy. Odds are, the moniker caught on because of the rich color that results when country ham, cured the right way for many months, meets hot black iron.

Look through the files of most country cooks and you'll never find a recipe for red-eye. Its ingredients are so few, its steps so simple, and its procedure so straightforward that creating a recipe was unnecessary—laughable even. Unlike many gravy recipes, there's not a speck of flour

*Beneath this Tennessee prosciutto is a layer of mayonnaise laced with redeye gravy, served at Rain in Abingdon, Virginia. Photo by Fred Sauceman.*

involved. Cooks don't expect it to be thick, and they know that, in the bowl on the table, it will separate into two-toned layers. Grease and water don't mix.

The simplicity of red-eye gravy reflects its origins in poverty. Other than the ham itself, the monetary investment is negligible. Made from the drippings of salty, cured ham, it has a highly concentrated flavor. Red-eye isn't eaten by the bowl but by the spoonful, over biscuits, grits, and potatoes.

Nowadays, people are looking anew at many staples of the Appalachian table. Ramps (wild mountain leeks), once maligned, are now heralded by hotshot chefs all over the country. Red-eye gravy, symbolic of making do during hard times, is likewise being reinterpreted.

Flipping through the Abingdon, Virginia, telephone directory, I noticed a menu for a restaurant on East Main Street called Rain. A couple of names caught my attention. One was Anson Mills, a company in Columbia, South Carolina, that turns heirloom varieties of corn into grits. The other was Benton, as in Allan Benton, curer of country ham and bacon in Madisonville, Tennessee. Allan's products are found throughout the menu at Rain. His bacon seasons Rain's shrimp and grits, and a recent special featured Benton's bacon with baked mussels, spinach, and Mornay sauce.

But what captured my attention in that telephone book ad was an appetizer: Benton's Tennessee prosciutto with "red-eye mayo" and scallions on a toasted baguette, eight dollars. And, yes, there was a little coffee in the mayonnaise.

*Rain*
*283 East Main Street*
*Abingdon VA*
*276-739-2331*

BUTTERMILK &
BIBLE BURGERS

# MILKING JERSEYS ON THE FRENCH BROAD

**IN HER NATIVE JAPAN, YUKI KOBAYASHI NEVER TASTED BUTTERMILK.** Now she helps produce it at a farm on the banks of the French Broad River in eastern Knox County, Tennessee.

After the devastating tsunami that hit Japan in March 2011, Colleen Cruze called up Google on her computer and searched for "Japanese Dairy Farm Intern."

Colleen, her brother and sister, and their parents, Earl and Cheri Cruze, milk a herd of about sixty Jersey cows whose milk contains the perfect percentage of butterfat for making ice cream. Cruze Dairy bottles whole milk, light milk, chocolate milk, and buttermilk and makes an ever-growing variety of ice creams.

*Yuki Kobayashi of Japan has learned the art and science of making ice cream at Cruze Dairy in Knox County, Tennessee. Photo by Larry Smith.*

"I heard on the news that the tsunami had hit an area in Japan where there were a lot of dairy farms," Colleen recalls. "I thought, if I could find a person from a dairy farm whose farm was ruined who could come here and help me get this work done, we would make a great team."

By 2013, three Japanese interns lived and worked on the Cruze farm. After studying agriculture at Big Bend Community College in Moses Lake, Washington, the interns relocated to East Tennessee for a fourteen-month experience. Their agriculture studies continue at the University of California-Davis.

Although Yuki was unfamiliar with buttermilk in Japan, she knew ice cream well. At Cruze, she calculates recipes and even develops new ones, including black sesame, a flavor reminiscent of her homeland.

When asked the secret of making good ice cream, Yuki says "love" and looks to Colleen for confirmation. "I hope to make ice cream in Japan," she adds.

The ice cream Yuki produces at Cruze is "from scratch," meaning it starts with the cracking of eggs and the making of custard and ends with a churn. Flavors include chocolate chip, strawberry-buttermilk, vanilla, and chocolate, with salty caramel being the most popular.

Earl Cruze is a fourth-generation dairy farmer. He has turned over much of the day-to-day work on the farm to Colleen, an agricultural sciences graduate of the University of Tennessee. Earl's trust in his daughter has never wavered, even after she ruined her first batch of buttermilk, all 500 gallons of it.

"He cried," says Colleen. "He was devastated for me. Luckily we have pigs, and we gave it to them. But he gave me another chance."

Naturally, there was a time in her life when Colleen wasn't sure the rigors and discipline of the dairy farm were for her. She felt a need to move away, to see the world. But eventually, the farm won out.

"What my parents started deserves to be kept going," she tells me. "Even on Christmas, those cows have to be milked twice a day. There's always more to do tomorrow on the farm. But it's a nice way to go to bed, knowing you have something to look forward to tomorrow."

Like Yuki, Colleen was a latecomer to drinking buttermilk. After years of encouragement, her father, Earl, hit upon the right approach. "I think that buttermilk you're drinking is making you prettier," he told her.

"And that was all he had to say to me to make me want to drink buttermilk," says Colleen.

Not only does she drink buttermilk regularly now; she also uses it as a facial mask.

"I figured since buttermilk is so good for you on the inside, it would be great for the outside, too," she says, laughing.

Colleen's husband, Manjit Bhatti, is from India. She says Cruze buttermilk is the perfect beverage to pair with foods from his homeland. "I drink buttermilk because I love spicy food, and it helps you to digest it. If I can eat more spicy, exciting foods, I'll drink more buttermilk."

*Colleen Cruze spends time with the herd on the family farm in Knox County, Tennessee. Photo by Larry Smith.*

Every Saturday during the warm months, the Cruze family brings a food truck to the Market Square Farmers Market in downtown Knoxville, where they cook Indian food with Southern on the side: curry and biscuits, for example. Indian mango lassi, made with East Tennessee buttermilk, is often on the menu, and Cruze Dairy makes a buttermilk-based lime-cardamom ice cream, featuring the popular Indian spice.

"We try to be as creative as we can with dairy products," Colleen says.

As the business has grown and the product line has expanded, the Cruze family never forgets to give credit to those who are most closely associated with the farm's success: the herd.

As Colleen affectionately puts it, "Those sweet brown cows with the big eyes."

## DESIGNER MOONSHINE?

**ONCE A SYMBOL OF MOUNTAIN REBELLION AND LAW-BREAKING ABANDON,** moonshine is becoming, well, almost genteel. NASCAR legend Junior Johnson, who served eleven months of a two-year sentence for running illegal liquor in the mid-1950s, is now co-owner of a completely legal and legitimate distillery in Madison, North Carolina, not far from where he once evaded law enforcement officers through wheel-screeching, middle-of-the-road U-turns in a car loaded with his daddy's moonshine.

Piedmont Distillers opened in 2005, and Junior joined as a partner two years later. The craft distillery's moonshine recipe, Midnight Moon, is one Junior learned from his father, Robert Lynn Johnson Sr.

"We triple-distill it, and it's got a real soft taste and not a burny taste," Junior tells me over a plate of barbecue and beans in a Tennessee hollow, where he has stopped to eat before an appearance at nearby Bristol Motor Speedway.

**BUTTERMILK &
BIBLE BURGERS**

*NASCAR legend Junior Johnson (right) used to run illegal whiskey through Bullock's Hollow near Bluff City, Tennessee, home of Ridgewood Barbecue, owned by Larry Proffitt (left) and his daughter, Lisa Proffitt Peters. Photo by Larry Smith.*

"My daddy always run 100 proof. Ours is eighty. We go up against them big-name vodkas and beat the fire out of them," says Junior, who grew up about ten miles outside North Wilkesboro, North Carolina. "We work them over now, I'll tell you. We've not come out with anything yet that didn't sell to the top of our expectations."

In February 2011, Piedmont introduced a line of "fruit inclusion spirits." Cherry, strawberry, and apple pie are the new flavors. Mason jars are hand-filled with fruit and Midnight Moon corn liquor.

"The ladies really like the apple pie," Junior notes. "We're in thirty-seven states now, and people up north, they're just drinking these products like the devil."

When Junior and his colleagues were in the market for a still, they visited Jack Daniel's in Tennessee and Jim Beam in Kentucky for ideas.

"Then we contacted a manufacturer, and three days later they called back and told us there was a still available in North Carolina, just like what we wanted. And built in 1930. And we went and hunted it down, and it was all copper. It didn't have no rust on it or nothing. We cleaned that booger up and set our fire and went to making liquor."

Junior Johnson was one of five inductees in the NASCAR Hall of Fame's inaugural class. He received a presidential pardon from Ronald Reagan in 1986 for his 1956 moonshining conviction.

## Midnight Moon and Lemonade

1½ ounces Midnight Moon over ice and fill with lemonade.

## Moonshine Martini

1½ ounces Midnight Moon and a splash of dry vermouth. Shake with ice and serve in a martini glass. Garnish with an olive or lemon peel.

## Midnight Moon and Tonic

1½ ounces Midnight Moon over ice and fill with tonic. Garnish with lime.

# A LATIN RIFF ON RAMPS

*Wild mountain leeks called ramps add personality to this West Virginia salsa. Photo by Fred Sauceman.*

**BRENDA DRENNEN'S RAMP REPERTOIRE IS EXTENSIVE.** When I talked to her one afternoon in late February, she was literally up to her elbows in the wild mountain leek, harvested near her home in Mount Nebo, West Virginia.

Especially through her sales and sampling sessions at Tamarack: The Best of West Virginia in Beckley, Brenda has become known for sometimes unpredictable treatments of the ramp, that unforgettable sign of spring in the Appalachian Mountains.

Emerald-hued ramp jelly and fluorescent ramp mustard join ramp vinaigrette dressing and hard-to-find jars of pickled ramps on the Tamarack shelf, all produced at the Farmer's Daughter, Brenda's business in Mount Nebo.

In 2008, she added a red product, ramp salsa.

"My husband, Jim, created it," Brenda tells me. "He loves ramps."

In addition to chip-dipping, Jim blends Farmer's Daughter ramp salsa into hamburger meat for grilling and laces his meatloaf with stout shots of it. And macaroni and cheese in the Drennen household has never been the same since Jim started topping it with ramp salsa.

"When we do tastings at Tamarack, people are so amazed," Brenda says. "The unique flavor of ramps really changes the salsa. Usually I encourage people to taste first, before they ask what's in there!"

# THE BANANA CROQUETTES OF KENTUCKY

**CONTEMPLATE KENTUCKY FOOD AND DRINK,** and the flagship products that immediately come to mind are hot brown sandwiches, corn pudding, country ham, and bourbon. But I discovered a latent banana mania in the Commonwealth.

When a Warren County cook spoke to me of banana croquettes in 2006, I envisioned fried patties of mashed banana, something on the order of the tostones of Puerto Rico—deep-fried plantains mashed in a wooden press. But I found that it was something different.

And the fried croquette typically made with salmon or chicken in the South bears absolutely no kinship to the treatment of bananas in the hands of Kentucky cooks. Unless you subscribe to the boiled dressing school, a Kentucky banana croquette is not cooked at all. There's not a single BTU of heat transfer involved.

For a classic Kentucky banana croquette, slice bananas, roll them in mayonnaise thinned with a little milk, and then roll them in crushed peanuts. Some call it "banana salad" and serve it on top of lettuce.

Judy Drury of Lexington, a Miracle-Whip-instead-of-mayonnaise activist, claims that few people under the age of fifty know of banana croquettes.

*Kentucky's love affair with the banana is long-standing.*

In Boston, Kentucky, they're paired with another food product that must travel a long way to get to the Bluegrass State: oysters. "These [banana croquettes] are on the traditional menu at Boston School's annual Oyster Supper," says Judy Richardson Jett. "This is the fall festival held by the PTA on the second Saturday in November to raise funds for the school."

One Kentucky cook I interviewed uses peanut butter as mortar to reassemble the sliced bananas before applying the mayonnaise dressing. A church cookbook from Williamstown replaces the outer coating of peanuts with crushed cornflakes.

For Christmas 1941, after Linda Ramsey Ashley's family had moved from Mt. Vernon to Frankfort so her father could lay bricks for a new state office building, Linda's mother made "banana salad," stood the bananas on the cut end, and "put a cherry on top," Linda says, "making rather lopsided candles."

For the family of Susan Meers Wells of Lexington, banana croquettes meant celebration and ritual.

"First, a grandchild was selected to have the honor of crushing the nuts. Whole peanuts were folded into a clean tea towel and sent to the front parlor hearth where they were then smashed to small chips with a heavy antique iron."

These two mismatched words, banana and croquette, bring forth food memories all over Kentucky. For a generation of cooks who hit their church supper stride around the middle of the last century, nothing said Kentucky cuisine any better than a dressed banana.

# The Gurneyburger House

## QUIRKYBURGERS

**THE OFFICE PHONE RANG SHORTLY BEFORE THREE-THIRTY ONE MARCH AFTERNOON.** It was
my colleague Jane MacMorran, on her way to a conference in Ohio. Stop-
ping off for a meal in Pikeville, Kentucky, she happened upon The Dairy
Cheer on South Mayo Trail.

Jane had taken my class, "The Foodways of Appalachia," back in 2006
and became a convert to Tootie-ism and a worshipper at the feet of pipe-
fitter Arvil Vance, creator of the Arvil Burger in Bristol, Tennessee. For
me, Tootie's, in business since 1945 in the Willie Boom community of
Bristol with its signature dish called the Arvil Burger, represented the ultimate confluence of weird nomenclature.

BUTTERMILK &
BIBLE BURGERS

*In the Happy Valley
community of East Tennessee,
there once was a Gurney
Burger, which captured
the attention of Charles
Kuralt of CBS News.
Photo by Fred Sauceman.*

But in my oddly named hamburger hall of fame, there was an empty corner: the southeastern section of Kentucky. Hence Jane's excitement. In Pikeville, she found the Smashburger, its name, I'd guess, derived from the whack of turner against raw meat against metal grill. The Smasharue, Jane told me, "was tastier with the addition of a cheese sauce with bacon bits. Neither burger was actually smashed as much as we had anticipated."

Arvil's burger lacks sauce and dramatic slapping noise, instead deriving its distinctiveness from its inside-out approach. Arvil packs the onions inside the patty. An unassuming man, Arvil would never willingly name a sandwich after himself, but when a friend tasted this hamburger inversion, he insisted that it carry the name of its inventor.

No study of hamburger terminology in the South would be complete without acknowledgment of the gone-but-not-forgotten Gurney Burger, named not for a hospital hallway item but rather for Gurney Campbell, who ran a place on the old Elizabethton highway in East Tennessee and another in Hampton. Gurney served a Pizza Burger, but it was his name-sake Gurney Burger that brought national attention to Johnson City on November 16, 1970, when reporter Charles Kuralt, in one of his "On the Road" segments during the *CBS Evening News,* said the following: "Old Gurney Campbell down there in Johnson City, Tennessee, couldn't resist naming his burger for himself. We have also consumed burgers from the grills of guys named Oliver, Buddy, Murray, Chuck, Ben, and Juan."

Like Gurney's, many offbeat hamburger names have nothing at all to do with taste or technique. The Big Hack at Clark's Grocery in Kingsport, Tennessee, is a memorial tribute to the late Hack Cleek, once the oldest chief of a volunteer fire department in Tennessee. My former student Laura Zuehsow tells me there's nothing out of the ordinary about what constitutes a Myrtle Burger at Jefferson Drug Store in Oak Ridge, Tennessee. It's a predictable meat-mustard-lettuce-onion-cheese combination, but customers swear it tastes like no other, and they attribute that special flavor to the chemistry created by the magical meeting of Myrtle Chapman's deft hands and freshly ground beef.

"I guess it's how I handle them," Myrtle told Laura, who was doing research for a class oral history project. "I pat them with love."

The disconnect between name and composition is most pronounced in northern Mississippi's slugburger. Never mind that a logo of the annual Slugburger Festival in Corinth, Mississippi, features a grinning gastropod. There's no snail in a slugburger. Its name dates to the Great Depression, when the word "slug" was slang for a nickel, and that was the burger's price. Although the slugburger name understandably never strayed far outside the Mississippi towns of Booneville and Corinth, the concept was universally applied in the Depression-era South: stretch more expensive meat with cheaper filler and dress it like a hamburger. Mustard, pickle, and onions are the standard slugburger condiments. Regina Smith at The White Trolley Café in Corinth taught me about slugburger doneness gradations. "I like them crisp," she said. "I don't like them soft." Regina added some over-the-lunch-counter philosophy: "You've got to taste them with an open mind."

Economic conditions didn't force Frederick "Pal" Barger to rethink the American hamburger at Pal's Sudden Service in the 1950s. Time-motion studies and temperature differentials forced his hand, resulting in what later came to be called the Sauceburger. As someone who compares making Big Pal hamburgers to assembling automobiles at GM, Pal evaluated the processes his employees were using and concluded that there were too many steps, so he created a mega-condiment mixture of ketchup, mustard, pickle relish, and spices, reducing the dressing of a hamburger to one step. And he warmed the sauce, curing the cold condiment on hot meat conundrum that Pal puzzled over when considering the traditional American hamburger. The renegade Sauceburger and the mainstream Big Pal helped the regional chain become America's first restaurant company ever to win the Malcolm Baldrige National Quality Award.

Then there are the hamburger poseurs. The Bologna Burger served at Elizabethton, Tennessee's Sycamore Drive-In sports all the predictable burger dressings but no ground beef. Owner Gary Hicks says he didn't want to call it a bologna sandwich because of the light-bread connotation. In Greeneville, Tennessee, the late Sonny Paxton made a good living selling Chipburgers, sandwiches of thinly sliced ham you ordered over a

*Although there's no snail in a Mississippi slugburger, promoters of the Slugburger Festival in Corinth have fun with the name. Logo courtesy the Slugburger Festival.*

telephone at the expansive Big Top on Summer Street, which now survives as the diminutive Little Top on North Main.

In naming their products, these burger purveyors haven't gone in for gentility or flowery language. In fact, some of the names they've come up with are downright unappetizing. The taste of the Cold Cold Heart Burger at The Burger Bar in Bristol, Virginia, far surpasses the sobering mystique of its name. But perhaps perverse delight is a strong promotional attraction. Other than honoring country music comedian Humphammer, of Bonnie Lou and Buster fame, why else would Gerry Neely be selling Humpburgers in Powell, Tennessee?

Pancho
Pit Cook for 24 Years
(1954 - 1988)

**Michael Booker** Our pit master joined us in 1974 - and he is truly the master of the hickory pit!

**Willie Morgan** Since 1988 Willie has smoked meat the Golden Rule way, the right way.

**Bernice Kelly**
Since 1945 Bernice has been cooking up Golden Rule's signature Bar-B-Q Baked Beans

**Peggy Martin** has been baking Golden Rule's world famous homemade pies since 1977.

Out of the rich folklore of Alabama comes the story of **The Original Golden Rule Bar-B-Q.** Since 1891, this roadside stop in a small town east of Birmingham was a favorite gathering spot for many a traveler going to and from Atlanta. The reason was the Golden Rule's legendary Bar-B-Q, slow cooked the old fashioned way over a real hickory pit and served with that uniquely sweet and spicy sauce. Travelers quickly spread the fame of Golden Rule Bar-B-Q across the Southeast. Rich and poor folk, celebrities and sports heroes made the pilgrimage to taste the "South's Most Famous Bar-B-Q" and many of their photos adorn our walls. As time passed the building was moved twice to accommodate modern highways and shopping centers, but thank goodness the Golden Rule folks never compromised their commitment to cooking Bar-B-Q **the old fashioned way.**

"The South's Most Famous Bar-B-Q"

**GOLDEN RULE.**
*Bar-B-Q and Grill*

# HIGH ON THE ALABAMA HOG

**"AND ON THE EIGHTH DAY WELL, YOU KNOW!"** reads a black-and-white bumper sticker from Dreamland Bar-B-Que. The age-old art and science of slow-cooking meat, or barbecue, is worshipped in the state of Alabama, from pecan-infused pork shoulder at Mobile's Brick Pit near the coast to white sauce-soaked chicken on the banks of the Tennessee River in the north central section of the state.

Alabama joins Arkansas, Georgia, South Carolina, North Carolina, Kentucky, and Tennessee in the Southern barbecue belt, a string of states whose styles of barbecue have influenced one another over the years. Birmingham is not always mentioned in a litany of America's barbecue

BUTTERMILK &
BIBLE BURGERS

*The Golden Rule in Irondale, Alabama, is one of the oldest barbecue restaurants in America, dating to 1891.
Photo by Fred Sauceman.*

meccas—Memphis, Kansas City, and Lexington, North Carolina, for example—but it was in and around Alabama's largest city where the Southern Foodways Alliance, headquartered at the University of Mississippi, chose to begin its "BBQ Trail," a collection of oral histories profiling the South's most storied barbecue establishments.

Amy Evans, oral historian for the alliance, describes Alabama as a "sponge, good at embracing other barbecue traditions." Alabama lies between the barbecue poles of Memphis and the Carolinas. Vinegar-based sauces akin to North Carolina varieties are found in northern Alabama, along with many variations of tomato-based sauces all over the state. Those sauces bear a kinship to the ones served in the barbecue houses of Memphis as well as across the state in East Tennessee.

South of Birmingham, vinegary sauces become scarce, while in eastern Alabama, mustard, a South Carolina influence, finds its way into spicy sauces, often in combination with tomato products.

An emblem of Alabama barbecue is a white sauce created by Robert "Big Bob" Gibson at his Decatur restaurant in 1925. Originally, cooks dunked chickens in the sauce. Employees joked that Big Bob's chickens were baptized in it. Gibson gave away the recipe freely, and it has been widely published in cookbooks and circulated on the Internet. Its dominant ingredients are mayonnaise, apple cider vinegar, lemon juice, black pepper, and salt.

The restaurant still operates today, run by Gibson's grandson Don McLemore and his son-in-law Chris Lilly. The sauce has evolved from a kitchen staple to a table condiment, and its use has expanded beyond chicken. Diners often bathe Big Bob Gibson's award-winning pork shoulder in it as well—the meat described by food critic Jeffrey Steingarten as among the "pinnacle of barbecue."

When *Southern Living* magazine created its barbecue map of the South in 1982, there was no acknowledgment of the white sauce, but by 2003, when the map was revised and reissued in *Southern Living Bar-B-Que: Our Ultimate Guide*, a large white bottle appeared over northern Alabama. Because of their many competition victories and television appearances, McLemore and Lilly have been described as "the rock stars of Alabama barbecue," and Big Bob's has now franchised into barbecue-crazed North Carolina. Gibson's is representative of the respect for tradition engendered by Alabama barbecue. It has been in the same family since 1925.

Although pipe-smoking patriarch John Bishop died in 1997, his family has not only kept his original Tuscaloosa DreamLand Bar-B-Que alive but has also expanded the restaurant into other Alabama cities such as Birmingham, Northport, Huntsville, Mobile, and even out of state into Georgia. Bishop presided over the pit in a redwood chair, and his early menu consisted of nothing more than ribs, white bread, chips, and drinks. A rib sandwich was three ribs atop commercial loaf bread. The sauce was, and still is, redolent of vinegar but with a tomato underpinning. Diners note the balance between the sour sauce and sweet ice tea, an accompaniment to barbecue throughout Alabama.

In the steel mill town of Bessemer, the Sykes family has been in the food business since 1956, first serving hamburgers, then converting to barbecue, still smoked in a pit inside the front door of the restaurant. Van Sykes, son of the original owner and current proprietor of Bob Sykes BarB-Q, summarized the philosophy of many Alabama barbecue pitmasters who are often asked for the "secret" of good barbecue.

"Not many people appreciate the dynamic of just salt, meat, and fire—that's it," Sykes told the Southern Foodways Alliance for its "BBQ Trail" website. "It's time-honored. Its genius is its simplicity."

Always respectful of tradition, Sykes once warned his employees that if a gas line were ever installed to replace the use of green hickory wood, he would "come back and haunt you." Sykes's sandwiches, like many across the state, can be stuffed with inside meat, the crust from the charred outside, or, as many diners prefer, a combination of the two.

Although not in the same family for the entire period, Irondale's Golden Rule is one of Alabama's oldest restaurants. It opened in 1891, a popular stop for barbecue and beer on Highway 78, the road to Atlanta. The Williams family started the business, and in the 1930s, electrician Jabo Stone married Ellene Williams. They ran the restaurant until 1969, when it was purchased by Michael Matsos, who had operated La Paree Restaurant and Michael's Sirloin Room in downtown Birmingham. The restaurant thus joined Pete's Famous Hot Dogs and Gus's Hot Dogs as part of Birmingham's Greek-owned restaurant community. Golden Rule's barbecue is started in a smoker that holds 600 pounds of meat at a time and then finished on a pit. The restaurant offers several styles of sauce that Matsos says have evolved as the franchise has grown throughout the South.

Demetri's BBQ in Birmingham is likewise Greek-owned. Sam Nakos carries on his father Demetri's legacy in hiring only Greeks to work as pit-masters on an open pit. The restaurant is also known for its fried pies.

Food historian John T. Edge has written, "In the South, barbecue is a civic religion. And a smoke-lacquered pig is a totem of shared faith." At Chuck's Bar-B-Q in the former mill town of Opelika, the connection between barbecue and religion is clear. Employees wear T-shirts with "Jesus, The Bread of Life" printed on the back, and beside the cash register, owner Chuck Ferrell's religious handouts proclaim "Something Better Than Barbecue."

Chuck's has been serving chopped pork butts since 1976, and the restaurant has popularized mustard-based barbecue sauce in that section of eastern Alabama. Over oak, hickory, and sometimes pecan wood, Ferrell smokes CT butt, a Boston butt with fat and bone removed. Sliced and chopped are serving options, as well as "chipped on the block," a finer cut and the owner's personal preference.

Ron Harwell, a contest representative with the Kansas City Barbeque Society and a resident of Decatur, Alabama, notes the prevalence of slaw as a topping for barbecue sandwiches in the state, while Amy Evans points to dill pickles as a defining condiment at places like the Green Top in Dora, open since 1951, where there is an assembly line of buns, barbecued pork shoulder, sauce, and a Tupperware bucket of pickles.

Alabama barbecuers like Dale Petit at the Top Hat in Blount Springs view the tending of the pits as a craft, not a job, says Evans. Petit arises at four-thirty in the morning to cut wood and make sauce.

Alabama barbecuers have come into the business through varied and circuitous routes. Chuck Ferrell once repaired looms. Leo Headrick, who opened the Green Top with his wife Susie, once mined coal. Rudolph McCollum, founder of Winfield's The Sparerib, spent thirty-two years as a schoolteacher in Fayette. The Boar's Butt in Winfield began as a barbecue stand operated by the local high school football coach. Gerald Atchison, owner of Sho'nuff BBQ in Alexander City, sold live bait before converting to barbecue. Bob Sykes sold bread.

They are representative of a legion of Alabama barbecue cooks who are committed to keeping a Southern tradition alive, despite modern-day pressures to take shortcuts. Among all the variations in cooking techniques, sauce ingredients, and side dishes, persistence and patience are their common characteristics.

Pride in their craft is evident, too, and chauvinistic slogans show it. A sign at Mobile's Brick Pit proclaims, "Welcome to the Best Damn Smoked Bar-B-Que in the Great State of Alabama," and crimson red signatures on the restaurant's walls echo the theme as diners create odes to the thirty-hour-smoldered meat. Of Dreamland's ribs, the restaurant's advertising asserts, "Ain't Nothing Like 'em Nowhere."

The late Alabama poet Jake Adam York, in "To the Unconverted," observed that "the joints rise through smoke and glow like roadhouses on Heaven's way. . . . Beef or pork, catfish, quail or armadillo, we've tried it all, loved it with brushes, kiss of vinegar, tongue of flame. . . ."

In Alabama, barbecue is ecumenical. It is both urban and rural, black and white, tomato-sweet and vinegar-sour, pulled and chopped. It is cinderblock simple and strip-mall slick. A product of the working class culture of the mills and factories, integrating all, it is one of the state's most unifying and enduring symbols.

Reprinted by permission from the *Encyclopedia of Alabama*. Copyright by the Alabama Humanities Foundation. www.EncyclopediaofAlabama.org.

# A CUBAN PIG ROAST IN EAST TENNESSEE

*Eduardo Zayas-Bazán
(standing in center) and
his family in Cuba.
Photo courtesy Eduardo
Zayas-Bazán.*

**ELENA ALLEN ADMITS TO COOKING CANNED BLACK BEANS.** But when her father, Eduardo Zayas-Bazán, travels each fall from Miami to Northeast Tennessee to roast a pig, soaking dried black beans overnight is the mandatory method.

Eduardo has honchoed a pig roast every year since 1971. Sour orange juice for the marinade is hen's-teeth scarce in the Tri-Cities. He makes do, as Cuban refugees always have. Grapefruit juice substitutes as a marinade for the pig. But cutting corners in a pot of black beans is out of the question.

"They simmer all day long," says Elena. "My sister-in-law Cindy cuts up all the onions and peppers. My dad puts in all of his touches. He's trying to teach the grandchildren, Lauren and Lindsey, to make the black beans, so they got to help a lot this year. It's spreading the family tradition. But I never can get them like he can. Every time we come to the pig roast, people say, 'These are the best black beans I've ever tasted.'"

Vinegar and Worcestershire sauce are Eduardo's additions. But a hefty measure of memory seasons the pot. Reminiscence surrounds the barbecue rig on this October day outside the Allandale Barn near Kingsport, Tennessee. The apparatus itself is a story.

"My Johnson City friend Dwight Runge, an American, grew up in Cuba," remembers Eduardo. "His father ran the largest textile firm in Cuba. At one time, Dwight's Spanish was better than his English, although he was of American parents. He grew up in the country in Cuba. That's where the textile plant was, in the countryside.

"And he loved pig roasts. So we got together in 1971 and decided we were going to do one. Together with Brook Stanley, an engineer, we came up with this contraption that we still use today."

Some describe it as a shoebox, others as a cake pan turned upside down. The iron grill that holds the pig sits on concrete blocks. Hot coals are shoveled underneath. Bricks anchor the aluminum foil insulation.

Ingenuity is applied to the marinating, too. Past pigs, studded with garlic and rubbed with oregano, have soaked all night in the bathtub, moistened with grapefruit juice, in the absence of *naranja agria*, sour orange. When the pig arrives in Kingsport frozen, an all-night, tepid water bath is in order.

The rig has made the rounds from campus religious centers at East Tennessee State University to the backyards of Eduardo's former neighbors on Johnson City's south side. The pig roast now takes place in Kingsport, home of Eduardo's daughter Elena and son-in-law Ed Allen.

"My parents just think I was born in East Tennessee, but I'm really Cuban," Ed jokes. "I think I've spent more time with my Cuban family than my East Tennessee family."

The Pedrosos, related by marriage to Eduardo, found Johnson City shortly after Fidel Castro's takeover in Cuba. The Veterans Administration Hospital at Mountain Home was in need of a urologist, and Dr. Roberto Pedroso took the job.

List Of Returning Captives

Continued on Page 6A, Col. 3

THE MIAMI NEWS

THE BEST NEWSPAPER UNDER THE SUN

Established In 1896          Miami, Fla., Thursday, April 12, 1962          Telephone FR 4-6211

*Eduardo Zayas-Bazán was a frogman in the Bay of Pigs Invasion. Image courtesy Eduardo Zayas-Bazán.*

Preparing side dishes for the pig roast, his daughter, Irene Pedroso Mitchell, consults the yellowed, olive oil-spotted, black composition book full of recipes her mother hustled out of Cuba. The family was allowed to take one bag out of the country. The book, full of recipes the family had hurriedly written down by hand, was placed in the bag, along with photo albums and the baptismal robe.

"I brought my mother Magdalena's congealed salad to this year's pig roast," Irene says. "It's an Americanized version, but mother made it in Cuba. It has American ingredients—fruit cocktail, cream cheese—but I took it right out of her recipe book. She bought the book at the Havana Woolworth's probably around 1960. Some of the pages you can hardly read for the grease."

Eduardo couldn't even smuggle a cookbook out of his home country. An attorney in Cuba, he was a frogman during the Bay of Pigs Invasion in 1961, was injured in the debacle, and imprisoned. After he fled to the U.S., he decided to teach, ultimately securing a job in the Department of Foreign Languages at ETSU and eventually becoming its chair.

At the annual Tennessee pig roast, Eduardo is amazed that the pig his family has obtained from Iowa, weighing in at 110 pounds dressed, cooks in just six hours.

"In Cuba, every time we went to the farm, if we happened to have a party, there was a pig roast," Eduardo remembers. "In my home province, Camagüey, the way we would do a pig roast would be in a very simple manner. We put it over a slow fire, in a hole, and it would take twelve to fifteen hours. We did not marinate the pig, although in other parts of Cuba, they did.

"I suppose one of the reasons pork was so popular in Cuba is that we had a lot of palm trees, and their fruit is very much edible for pigs. As part of our diet, it was important to have pork on a weekly basis, some people on a daily basis."

Eduardo's son Eddy is now tender of the fire. Near the roasting pig, a ring of bricks encircles a pyramid of charcoal, and the fiery symmetry suggests an old ritual. Eddy shovels graying coals under the pig almost hourly, careful to concentrate more heat beneath the garlic-studded hams, which take longest to cook.

"If you get too many flames, you know something's wrong," advises Eddy. "It's tricky at first. If it's too hot, you'll burn the skin and you won't have the cracklings that everybody likes."

"We are partial to the skin," echoes his father. "That's something not typical even of American barbecue, but to us, the skin is a delicacy. And of course I love the tenderloin and the ribs. I love pigs' feet, but you don't eat the feet of the pig when you do a pig roast."

To describe the event, Eduardo's wife Lourdes prefers the Spanish term, *lechón asado*. "When you write about this, you need to call it *lechón* because 'pig' is too vulgar," she insists.

Young pig is preferable for roasting because of its leanness. This one was placed over the fire at ten minutes past eleven in the morning, and at five-thirty in the afternoon, Eddy pronounced it done.

"Another five minutes and we'd have been in trouble."

Sensing that the pig is about to be unveiled, guests ease closer to the fire. Without any instruction, male family members pull on gloves and line up around the cooker like pallbearers. The top is hoisted off, and Cubans stop conversation in mid-story to crack off hunks of skin. The men claim their spots around a picnic table. There's an obvious and understood division of labor.

"Ed and my father get the hams and we start processing," says Eddy. "And Sam Mitchell also helps to cut. Usually we have two or three who cut. Every year we lose a knife.

"We try to get it going fast because people don't like to sit around and wait. They're ready. We try to do a little socializing up front, and then it's all business when we cut the pig."

*Eduardo Zayas-Bazán (right) and Dwight Runge roast a pig, Cuban-style, in Johnson City, Tennessee, in 1971. Photo courtesy Eduardo Zayas-Bazán.*

"Here he comes, the grand master," says Ed Williams, a former ETSU colleague, as his friend Eduardo approaches the carving table. "You've never had to sit down to do the carving before, Eduardo. But that's what happens to us all, isn't it?"

"Do we have a scrap table yet, Eddy?" Sam Mitchell asks. "Keep a cold drink so you can cool that hand off."

"Eddy, you need to cut things in bigger pieces," Eduardo coaches his son.

"There's a good piece of skin right there, next to the side meat," Eddy tells his father. "I think this pig turned out very good. I think it's better than last year's. I really do. This is like a traditional Christmas Eve dinner in Latin and Hispanic culture, *Noche Buena*. In Cuban culture, it's all about the family and tradition and passing it on to future generations."

"The pig is always smiling," Ed Allen jokes. "Eduardo saves the heads and mounts them on his wall."

Grandchildren pose for pictures with the pig's head.

Surrounded by plates full of salted and olive-oiled white rice, oregano-perfumed black beans, and strips of the precious pork, Eduardo pushes back from the table and engages in some professorial analysis.

"The pig turned out very well. Everything is perfectly cooked, and the flavor, from what I have tasted, is terrific, so we're delighted. This may be the best yet."

Dr. Gonzalo Pedroso, Irene's grandfather, was a urologist in Cuba. Before Castro, the urology ward of the main hospital in Havana was named after him. Dr. Pedroso was also known for his culinary skills. The story goes that Fulgencio Batista, the Cuban president before Castro, asked to be invited to eat a meal prepared by the doctor. Dr. Pedroso told the president, however, that he did not want to invite him because of the entourage that would come along. The incident became a symbol of the freedom of the Cuban medical community from political interference, although that had not been Dr. Pedroso's original intent. His black bean recipe is on the facing page.

# Cuban Black Bean Stew

| | | | |
|---|---|---|---|
| 2 | cups dry black beans | 2 | bay leaves |
| 4 | garlic cloves, chopped | 2 | medium onions, chopped |
| 1 | green bell pepper, chopped | 1/2 | cup olive oil |
| 1 1/2 | tablespoons sugar | 2 | tablespoons vinegar |
| 2-3 | dashes Tabasco | 2 | teaspoons Worcestershire sauce |
| 1/4 | teaspoon oregano | 2 | teaspoons salt |
| 1/4 | teaspoon black pepper | | |

*Rinse beans with cold water to clean. Place in 4-quart Dutch oven and cover with water until there is about 2 inches of water over beans.*

*Bring to a boil; simmer for 2 minutes, and let stand, covered, for 2 hours.*

*Add bay leaves, bring to a boil, and simmer for 1 1/2 to 2 hours or until beans are tender.*

*Sauté onions, garlic, and bell pepper in olive oil until limp, not letting vegetables brown, about 15-20 minutes.*

*Add to beans with rest of ingredients. Bring to a boil, mash some of the beans to thicken stew, and simmer 30-40 minutes or until thick.*

*Serve over cooked white rice. Serves 10-12.*

# A TASTE OF HUNGARY IN THE HILLS

**THE SPIRITS OF HUNGARIAN GRANDMOTHERS INFUSE THE KITCHEN** and fellowship hall of St. Elizabeth's Catholic Church in Pocahontas, Virginia, from early morning until late afternoon on two October Saturdays.

Parishioners feel the presence of their ancestors as cabbage heads boil in vats and paprika-seasoned onions fry in butter.

As dangerous and demanding as work in a coal mine was, Hungarians saw it as a way out, a path to something better, and they made their way from Europe to this tiny town on the Virginia-West Virginia line, beginning in the late nineteenth century.

"Conditions were very bad in Hungary at that time," says church member Andrew Satmary. "Hungarians came here in hopes that they could make some money and eventually go back home."

BUTTERMILK &
BIBLE BURGERS

*Erika Lavender, born in Germany, chops the "trash" while she cooks onions in paprika for Hungarian cabbage rolls in Pocahontas, Virginia. Photo by Fred Sauceman.*

Andrew's mother made the long journey from Austria-Hungary to the mountains of Virginia in 1898, two years after the founding of St. Elizabeth's, a Catholic church built to meet the spiritual needs of people from all over Europe, in a largely Protestant region of America.

"She did not come through Ellis Island," Andrew tells me as we talk in the fellowship hall of the tiny church he has attended all his life. "My mother and grandmother came through Norfolk, Virginia."

*St. Elizabeth's Catholic Church in Pocahontas, Virginia, was founded in 1896. Photo by Fred Sauceman.*

No doubt most of the miners who migrated to Virginia toward the close of the nineteenth century knew about what had happened on March 13, 1884. On that day, 114 miners were killed in the east mine of the Southwest Virginia Improvement Company. A 1984 monument marks their mass grave in Pocahontas Cemetery, a multiethnic burying ground carved, grave by grave, out of a steep hillside.

Knowledge of that accident notwithstanding, Germans, Poles, Slavs, and people from throughout the Austro-Hungarian Empire moved into boardinghouses in Pocahontas, a town whose population has now declined to about 400.

Barbara Jones Drosick's grandparents came to Pocahontas from Budapest and secured a house next to one owned by the coal company.

"Grandmother Drosick took care of boarders who worked in the mines," Barbara says. "She was a breadmaker. She made round pones of bread and sold them. And she made her own chicken noodle soup and her own noodles."

Steve Danko, of nearby Bluefield, Virginia, says his Hungarian immigrant ancestors were master soup makers.

"In those days, you only got paid for coal that you mined. You did not get paid for the rock. You could work all day long moving rock with a pick and shovel and not get paid for it. Soup and noodles could feed a lot of people, on just a little money."

No matter what the weekly income was, though, Hungarians in Southwest Virginia managed to come up with the ingredients for cabbage rolls.

"You weren't a good Hungarian family if you didn't have cabbage rolls on Sunday," Andrew Satmary remembers. "We didn't feel like we had a meal if we didn't have cabbage rolls."

Stuffed with ground pork, rice, buttery onions, and paprika, cabbage rolls have been served at St. Elizabeth's for around sixty-five years. Now, instead of a fellowship hall dine-in, church members assemble and sell them, twelve to a plastic bag, for carryout only. Between those two Saturdays, more than 5,000 cabbage rolls go out the door.

Donna Lambert says you'd be surprised to know where all those cabbage rolls are going: Bluefield, Tazewell, Richlands, Grundy, Wytheville, across the state line into West Virginia, and even to Florida.

Donna's job is to count, to make sure every ziplock bag contains exactly a dozen rolls and that every customer gets a bag of "trash." Those are scraps of cabbage used to line the bottom of the pot so the rolls, when boiled in tomato juice at home, won't burn.

*On a hill overlooking Pocahontas, Virginia, St. Elizabeth's Catholic Church is infused with the smells of garlic, pork, cabbage, paprika, and onions every October. Photo by Fred Sauceman.*

Erika Lavender, originally from Germany, chops up the trash while she cooks the onions and paprika for the filling. "In Germany," she says, "we added sauerkraut. But everybody fixes them differently." In the Satmary household, cabbage rolls were always tinged with garlic.

Andrew Satmary's job in the church kitchen is to core the cabbage, and his octogenarian hands are still limber enough to make quick work of the assignment. Each church member has a specific job on these fall Saturdays. Men tend the boiling pots of cabbage. Women stuff the pork mixture into the leaves and roll them. No one complains about the hot, hard work.

"This is more about fellowship than money," Andrew says. "Years ago we had a grape festival. We'd get a good gypsy band out of Ohio, dance and have a good time. There were grapes hanging up, and if you stole some for your girlfriend, you had to pay a price."

Despite the upsurge in demand for cabbage rolls, parishioners aren't sure how long the old-country tradition of making them will continue in Pocahontas.

Says Frances Borbas, whose parents were both Hungarian, "The older women taught us everything we know, and there's just not that many of us anymore to do this."

But considering the shared inheritance of tenacity that has come down through the bloodlines of Eastern Europe to the mining territory of Southwest Virginia, perpetuating the cabbage roll is an odds-on certainty.

## NOBLE NOODLES

*The Jonesborough Kiwanis Club, in Tennessee's oldest town, is known for its annual spaghetti feast, but the sauce is a well-guarded secret. Photo by Fred Sauceman.*

**THE JONESBOROUGH KIWANIS CLUB ISN'T LARGE.** Its membership roster lists about forty people. They gather every Tuesday morning at the town's Senior Center on Persimmon Ridge Road in Tennessee's oldest town. They quaff a little coffee, trade some friendly barbs with a member whose attendance may have slipped, handle some club business, and host a speaker.

But the laid-back give-and-take of those early morning meetings is deceptive. These Kiwanians, some long retired, some a long way from it, spread good will and good works all over Washington County.

In a year's time, they manage to raise about $20,000. They help students in the county work toward better grades. Their presence is felt on Little League baseball diamonds and youth soccer fields. The Community Help Center in Sulphur Springs benefits from Jonesborough Kiwanis largesse. The Salvation Army is touched by this little club. The Second Harvest Food Bank relies on it.

Much of that yearly total is taken in through the activities of one day. It's a mid-winter tradition that many Washington Countians would not miss: the Annual Spaghetti Dinner, held at the Jonesborough Middle School.

Pat Wolfe, a member of the Jonesborough Kiwanis Club and also a Washington County commissioner, says it takes about fifty people to put on the event: club members, spouses, the Kiwanis Builders Club at Grandview School, and staff at the Jonesborough Senior Center who handle cake-baking duties.

The centerpiece of the event is sauce. It's a mysterious, storied sauce. Its creator was the late Judson Thornton, a local lawyer who was so secretive with the recipe that you'd think it was protected by attorney-client privilege.

Pat Wolfe says the sauce recipe is as confidential as anything created by Colonel Sanders. "Both of Judson's daughters know it, as well as one other person," he adds.

The mantle of sauce-making has fallen on Lloyd Fleenor, a retired insurer and realtor.

To go with Judson Thornton's tenacious sauce, club members boil up some 125 pounds of noodles, beginning around ten-thirty in the morning the day of the dinner. Garlic bread, salad, and drink round out the community feast.

Pat tells me this dinner has been going on for about a half a century now. "It was first held years ago at the Jonesborough United Methodist Church, and then, as it started to grow, it was moved to the Jonesborough Middle School."

Now, it's the Jonesborough Kiwanis Club's largest single fund-raising project, even though the all-you-can-eat price is amazingly low.

I wouldn't miss it. It's noodles for a noble cause.

## RAINBOWS AT SUNBURST

**NEARING NINETY, DICK JENNINGS IS STILL LOOKING TO THE FUTURE.** As he and his daughter Sally Eason walk alongside the fish-filled raceways at their family business, Sunburst Trout, near Canton, North Carolina, Dick stops.

"We need to know more about the smoking industry," Dick tells his daughter emphatically. "And I want you, if you possibly can, to get on your computer and dig up some information about smokers, what their trade journal is, get a subscription, consider putting an ad in it, and see if they don't have a convention somewhere that we can go to. We could double that business."

"I'll get right on it," Sally answers.

BUTTERMILK &
BIBLE BURGERS

*"I was the first person in the Southeast to raise fish of any kind for commercial purposes," says Dick Jennings. Photo courtesy Sally Eason.*

World War II prevented Dick from getting an engineering degree, but you could never tell it. He has an engineer's mind, and it shows in his carefully worded, thoughtful, and visionary language, in his knowledge of systems and how they work, and in his curiosity about the world.

Born in Pittsburgh, Pennsylvania, in 1924 to a family of privilege, Dick has made a life in the mountains of North Carolina. His grandfather, oilman E. H. Jennings, bought 35,000 acres in Jackson County in 1895.

*The Jennings and Eason families have overcome more than their share of hardships to keep Sunburst Trout going. Photo by Fred Sauceman.*

"About that time, the Vanderbilts were acquiring property in Asheville," says Thomas Bates, vice president of Lonesome Valley Development in Sapphire, North Carolina, a company that has transformed the remaining 800 acres of the Jennings property into a rural residential community of forests, pasture, streams, and pond at the base of Laurel Knob, a 1,200-foot wall of granite.

It was on this property where Dick launched his first North Carolina business venture, a mink farm. "I thought that filled the bill," Dick tells me, "but mink and fancy, elegant fur went out of style within twenty years."

A trout farm, says Thomas Bates, "was established here as a food supply for the mink."

Seeing no future in furs, Dick first started selling trout to stock small ponds for recreational fishing in East Tennessee, northern South Carolina, northern Georgia, Alabama, Virginia, and Kentucky. He was the first person in the Southeast to raise fish of any kind for commercial purposes.

When Dick first began to sell trout to restaurants, his methods, he admits, were sometimes "primitive." The Gerber baby food company furnished him with tin cans free of charge. He would put fish into those cans with, he says, "a little wet ice," and load them onto a bus bound for Atlanta, where he had a colleague waiting to take the product around the city.

Jennings Trout eventually became Sunburst Trout at its present location on property once owned by Canton's Champion Paper Company. The area was known as the Sunburst logging community, and Sally Eason

BUTTERMILK & BIBLE BURGERS

thought it would be a perfect new name for the family business. In fact, she says the color of the trout filets produced in the Haywood County location reminds her of a sunburst.

Filets make up about sixty percent of Sunburst's business today. Since 1985, the company has expanded to offer some fifteen value-added products. The first was smoked trout, done off the back of a tractor-trailer rig. Sally calls it "one of Dad's many engineering feats."

Figuring out a way to make use of the small pieces of fish that fell off the smoker rack, the family created a trout dip. Then came cold-smoked trout, which involved extensive research and trips to Europe to learn the fine points of the technique.

In 2006, Sunburst hired a research and development chef, Charles Hudson, who has added to the product line by developing a trout jerky.

*Trout caviar was once discarded as a nuisance at Sunburst. Now it's a vital part of this North Carolina business. Photo by Fred Sauceman.*

Sunburst employees carry the jerky with them all the time for a quick snack that does not need refrigeration.

Trout caviar, once thrown away and viewed as a nuisance, has become a big seller at Sunburst, catching the attention of chefs like Jacques Pépin.

"The egg pops in your mouth, with just the right texture," he says, before preparing a potato pancake, spreading it with Sunburst trout caviar, spooning sour cream into the middle, and sprinkling the dish with chives. He cuts the pancake into wedges as a first course.

"I appreciate all farmers and all people like Sally who grow things out of the earth, because too much has been said about the chef and not enough about the farmer," says Jacques Pépin. "We would be nothing without people like this."

Jacques Pépin's words are especially meaningful to the Jennings and Eason families, who have overcome more than their share of hardships to keep their business going. In 1986, water temperatures reached seventy-three degrees, a lethal level for trout, and all the fish at Sunburst perished within forty-eight hours.

"That's one more disaster than we're willing to take on, we thought," says Sally. "But after about a month, we changed our minds."

In 2004, two hurricanes swept through western North Carolina, ten days apart. Flooding and drought are constant threats. And in 2006, the business fell victim to arson. Yet the family keeps on.

"I think as a farmer that my responsibility is to my customers and to this land so that when I leave it, it's in as good a shape if not better than when I came," says Sally.

Case in point: The water at Sunburst emerges out of the Pisgah National Forest and is channeled into manmade Lake Logan. From there it is piped into the Sunburst system at some 12,000 gallons a minute, courses through a tier of raceways, undergoes purification, and then reenters the Pigeon River.

"So we borrow the water and then return it," Sally says. "It's just ultra-pure."

Adds Dick Jennings, "Because trout is a delicate, sensitive animal just like its taste, it has to have optimum conditions to survive."

Even in death, trout from the Sunburst waters have a recurring effect on Haywood County. The compost system at Sunburst, funded by a local company, Mountain Organics, enriches gardens all around.

"We compost all of our waste," says Sally. "It makes fabulous fertilizer. We sell it by the backhoe scoop to local farmers. They love it. It grows huge vegetables."

Dick, Sally, her husband Steve, and their children and grandchildren watch their trout come full circle. The family converted the barn on the original Jackson County property Dick's grandfather bought in 1895 into a restaurant called Canyon Kitchen. It is overseen by native North Carolinian John Fleer, a graduate of the Culinary Institute of America. Sunburst trout, less than a day out of the water, is a menu centerpiece.

"I love seeing the mix of people in the restaurant," says John. "Some come in shorts and sandals, and some come in pearls and dressed to the nines. Nature is our décor. We throw open the doors at night and feel the cross-breeze from the mountains."

Dick Jennings's father once warned him not to stay in the North Carolina mountains. He would starve, his father predicted. Instead, Dick and his family prospered, largely through the persistence and determination they learned firsthand from their neighbors in Appalachia.

 ## Lime-Basil Grilled Trout Filets

4  Sunburst trout filets

Juice of 1 lime

One handful of fresh basil leaves (about 1 ounce), chopped

2  cloves garlic, minced

1/4  cup olive oil

1  teaspoon Lawry's Seasoned Salt

1  teaspoon freshly ground black pepper

*Make a marinade by mixing the lime juice, basil, garlic, olive oil, seasoned salt, and pepper.*

*Marinate the trout for at least an hour.*

*Remove trout from marinade and place on a well-oiled, pre-heated grill.*

*Start flesh side down for about 3 minutes and then flip for another 2-3 minutes of cooking. Serves 4.*

# SORGHUM, A SWEETENER OF HISTORIC PROPORTIONS

**WHEN KENTUCKIAN JANICE SHELTON SITS DOWN FOR BREAKFAST** at The Farmer's Daughter in Chuckey, Tennessee, she immediately squeezes a puddle of sorghum syrup onto her plate and carves out a hunk of butter. The elbows of the former basketball coach fly as she vigorously mixes these two farm products for her biscuits.

Janice's home state of Kentucky and her adopted state of Tennessee lead the country in the production of sorghum syrup. But The Farmer's Daughter is one of the few restaurants where it's always on the table, thanks to local producers Arland and Novella Johnson, owners of Johnson's Sweet Sorghum in Limestone.

*Sorghum is a main ingredient in the dried apple stack cake recipe Jill Sauceman learned from her grandmother, Nevada Parker Derting, in Scott County, Virginia. Photo by Larry Smith.*

Growing a field of cane, harvesting it, squeezing out the juice, and boiling that juice down into a rich, thick liquid is hard work. It burns easily, the sugars can get out of balance, and the green taste is difficult to remove. But the laborious enterprise doesn't seem to be dying away.

The National Sweet Sorghum Producers and Processors Association—yes, there is a professional organization for sorghum people—gave me an encouraging statistic recently. Since 2001, membership in the NSSPPA has grown five-fold, from 110 to 550, in forty-one states.

We've been eating sorghum in America since colonial times but have been producing it ourselves only since the 1850s, when the cane completed its route from Africa to Europe to North America. The word "sorghum," like the cane itself, has African origins.

The pure syrup is a good source of iron and potassium. Before the era of vitamins, doctors prescribed it for nutrient-deficient patients.

At times in our history when sugar prices soared, sorghum was often relied on as a primary sweetener. During the Civil War, it was rationed to soldiers. A Columbia, South Carolina, prisoner-of-war enclave came to be known as "Camp Sorghum," since Union prisoners were given rations of the syrup, along with cornmeal.

Other than an unadulterated squeeze on the finger, sorghum's most pervasive use in the South is a coupling with cornbread or biscuits. At our house, glugs of it sweeten my wife Jill's dried apple stack cake, made from a recipe used by her family in Southwest Virginia for well over 100 years.

As I was having breakfast at The Farmer's Daughter with Janice Shelton and her friends from Johnson City's Central Baptist Church, the inevitable question arose: what is the difference between sorghum and molasses? I've been on a campaign of late to clear up the confusion, for they are two different products.

"Molasses is a by-product of the making of sugar, and sugar cane will not grow in this area," says Arland Johnson. "Molasses can even be a blended product and can contain as much as twenty percent Karo syrup. Even your sugar people, way down South, if they make a pure syrup from sugar cane, they don't call it molasses. They call it ribbon cane syrup."

Arland describes his sorghum syrup as "Mother Nature in a jug," since it contains no additives whatsoever. It's readily available near the produce sections of area Food City stores. At Christmastime, it is commonly used in the making of gingerbread and ginger cookies. In the Johnson household, sorghum is mixed into peanut butter, baked beans, and barbecue sauce.

One of the largest sorghum producers in Tennessee is Muddy Pond in Overton County, with a yield of about 8,000 gallons a year. Owner Mark Guenther, of Canadian extraction, swabs it over pizza, blends it into venison bologna, and constructs a sandwich of sorghum-smeared bread, peanut butter, tomato, and mayonnaise. He's proud of his product.

Arland and Mark are thankful for this simple grass and for those who had the good sense, a long time ago and a long way away, to extract its precious juice, apply heat, and revel in the results.

 ## Nevada Parker Derting's Stack Cake

| | |
|---|---|
| 1 | pound dried tart apples |
| 1/2 | cup sorghum |
| 1/2 | cup sugar |
| 1/2 | cup buttermilk |
| 1 | egg |
| 1 | teaspoon baking soda |
| 1 | teaspoon baking powder |
| 1/2 | teaspoon salt |
| 1/3 | cup shortening |
| 4 1/2 | cups (approx.) of White Lily flour, plus enough for flouring the board when rolling out each layer. |

*This is our most requested recipe. Notice that it includes no spicing.*

*Cover dried apples with water, and cook over medium-low heat until most of the water is absorbed and the apples break up when stirred. If apples are not soft enough to break up, add more water and keep cooking. If desired, add a tablespoon or so of sugar to taste.*

*Cool and run apples through a sieve or Foley Food Mill to produce a smooth sauce. Meanwhile, combine the remaining ingredients. Dough should be the consistency of stiff cookie dough.*

*Separate dough into five to seven balls. Roll each ball of dough to a 1/8- or 1/4-inch thickness. Cut into 8- or 9-inch rounds. (Nevada Derting used a pie pan with a scalloped edge to cut out rounds.)*

*Prick each layer with a fork, making a nice design. Sprinkle individual layers with granulated sugar and bake on a greased cookie sheet at 400 degrees until golden brown (about 5–8 minutes, depending on thickness). (Mrs. Derting sometimes baked hers in iron skillets.)*

*Cool and place the first layer on a cake plate. Spread a coating of cooked apples over the layer, within half an inch of the edge.*

*Stack the other layers, alternating cake and cooked apples and ending with a cake layer on top. Save the layer with the prettiest design for the top.*

*Store, covered, in a cool place for several days before serving.*

# A CENTERPIECE OF ALABAMA CELEBRATIONS

**PARTICIPATING IN A BANNED BOOKS WEEK READING OF HARPER LEE'S** remarkable novel *To Kill a Mockingbird* reminded me of the many food references in that book. When Aunt Alexandra comes to live with the Finch family, Miss Maudie Atkinson bakes a Lane cake to welcome her. Noting the cake's alcoholic kick, the character Scout remarks, "Miss Maudie baked a Lane cake so loaded with shinny it made me tight."

The names of the creators and inventors of many of our dishes in the South have been lost to time. Not so with the Lane cake. We know exactly whom to credit: Emma Rylander Lane.

Mrs. Lane wasn't a self-promoter. She had to be convinced that her cake creation should bear her last name. At first, it was called the Prize

*Emma Rylander Lane created the Lane cake in the late 19th century. Photo by Neil Ravenna.*

cake, since it had captured first place in a baking contest at a county fair in Columbus, Georgia, where Mrs. Lane was demonstrating ranges. Her cake, Mrs. Lane wrote, was "named not from my own conceit, but through the courtesy of Mrs. Janie McDowell Pruett, of Eufaula, Ala."

My friend John Egerton, who literally wrote the book on Southern food, says that the first time he baked a Lane cake, he was in the kitchen three hours.

It's a type of sponge cake, made in layers, with a filling of butter, raisins, and whiskey and a boiled, fluffy white frosting of water, sugar, and whipped egg white. For over a century, it has been a special occasion cake in the South and the pride of the state of Alabama.

In addition to the richness of the ingredients, part of its allure is its flirtation with the forbidden. Especially in the dry counties of Alabama, feasting on a whiskey-laced dessert was an adventure on the wild side. Home bakers who have objected to the whiskey or brandy in the original recipe have substituted grape juice, especially for children's birthdays.

The recipe was first printed in Mrs. Lane's book *Some Good Things to Eat*, which she self-published in 1898. It has been modified in many ways over the years. Coconut, dried fruit, and nuts are common additions, but they are not included in the original recipe.

Mrs. Lane, who died in 1904, instructed that the Lane cake be made not in cake pans but in pie tins. She specified "one wine-glass of good whiskey or brandy" for the filling and insisted that the icing be tested with a clean spoon. The raisins were to be "finely clipped."

"The layers make the cake, not the icing," says Alabama chef Neil Ravenna. "The cake itself is made with egg whites, almost like a sponge cake, so it will soak up all the bourbon and all the other wonderfully tasting things in there."

Most bakers agree that the Lane cake is best if made a day or so in advance of serving, to allow those flavors to blend.

In Alabama and throughout the South, the baking of an elegant, scratch-made, laborious Lane cake is a sign that a noteworthy life event is about to be celebrated. Chef Ravenna shared Mrs. Lane's recipe with me.

 # Lane Cake

3 ¼   cups sifted flour

2   teaspoons baking powder

1   cup butter

2   cups sifted sugar

1   cup sweet milk

8   egg whites

1   tablespoon vanilla

*Sift the flour and baking powder together three times.*

*Cream the butter and sugar until perfectly light. Add to it alternately, a little at a time, milk and flour, until all are used, beginning and ending with flour. Last, beat in the well-whipped whites and vanilla. Bake in four layers, using medium-sized pie tins, with one layer of ungreased brown paper in the bottom of each tin.*

***Filling:*** *Beat well together 8 egg yolks, one large cup of sugar, and half a cup of butter. Pour into a small, deep stew pan and cook on top of the stove until quite thick, stirring all the time, or it will be sure to burn. When done and while still hot, put in one cup of seeded and finely clipped raisins, one wine-glass of good whiskey or brandy, and one teaspoon of vanilla. Spread thickly between the layers and ice. It is much better to be made a day or two before using.*

***Icing:*** *White of 1 egg, 1 cup granulated sugar, 4 tablespoons boiling water. Put sugar into a perfectly clean, bright pan. Pour the boiling water over it, put it on a hot fire, and stir carefully back and forth (not round and round as that will make the icing grain) until the sugar is all dissolved. Remove the spoon, wash it clean, dry it, and when the icing has boiled a few minutes dip up a spoonful and pour it back slowly, and if it runs from the spoon in a fine thread it is done. Take it from the stove and pour it slowly on the well-whipped egg white, beating carefully as you pour, and continue beating until it is cool. Flavor to taste, and if the icing runs, put in a pinch of tartaric acid.*

# PART THREE
# THE PLACES

# KNOXVILLE SHAKES AT LONG'S

**THE LIGHTS OFFICIALLY COME ON AT LONG'S DRUG STORE** in Knoxville, Tennessee, at eight o'clock in the morning. But customers ignore that obvious signal of the beginning of the business day. In the unlit building in the Kingston Pike Shopping Center, activity commences long before the appointed hour.

Customers pour coffee for each other. They rearrange tables. Some businesses might view the early morning commotion as a violation of protocol. Not so at Long's. Helping yourself and reconfiguring furniture only mean one thing to owner Hank Peck and his father Jim. It's a sign that customers feel at home.

*Hank Peck and his father Jim have kept pharmacy and food in the family. Photo by Fred Sauceman.*

*Ruth Pate has been working at Long's since the late 1970s. Photo by Fred Sauceman.*

"This is like the biggest kitchen in Knoxville," says Hank. "It has always been a meeting place for different people."

Mary Constantine, food writer for the *Knoxville News Sentinel*, says Long's is where the city's "movers and shakers" gather.

"Just about every mayor we've had has eaten here," says Jim, who is well past eighty and still practicing pharmacy. "Senator Howard Baker ate here. Dolly Parton and her sister used to come in here. Peyton and Archie Manning. Actress Patricia Neal."

On the day of my last visit, the University of Tennessee Lady Vol basketball coaching staff occupied the counter stools. Bobby Scott, one of the greatest quarterbacks in UT football history, stopped in, too. Jim says General Robert Neyland, the legendary coach for whom the stadium at Tennessee is named, got his prescriptions filled at Long's.

"Our clientele has always been a respectable bunch, a sophisticated bunch," says Jim, who started working at Long's in 1959, just three years after its opening.

"In the early 1960s, there were sit-ins on Gay Street downtown," Jim recalls. "One day seventeen students from Knoxville College [a historically black institution] came into the drugstore. I told the staff that the door was unlocked and they should go wait on them."

At that time, before the construction of West Town Mall, Long's was, as Jim describes it, "at the end of the world, right at the Knoxville city limits."

At one time, Clarence "Doc" Long owned four drug stores. After Long was killed in a car accident in 1966, his wife sold all four. Today's Long's was the last to sell.

"There was never a thought about changing the name," Jim Peck tells me. "Dr. Long did it right. Everybody loved him. He had a good way about him."

The current owners continue that tradition of hospitality. One visit to Long's and you feel like a regular.

"My father is the biggest cutup you've ever seen in your life," Hank says. "Doc Long was the same way."

Jim tells me about the time he "prescribed" repeated doses of vodka and orange juice for a former UT football player who had been stung by yellow jackets and how the player fumbled for an explanation for his intoxication when his wife found out.

The Peck family's sense of humor and respect for others are reflected in the longevity of the employees who serve three meals a day at the drugstore. Ruth Pate has been working at Long's for thirty-four years. She helped open Knoxville's first Krispy Kreme doughnut store, cleaned motel rooms, and then found a home at Long's.

In hiring Ruth, Hank and Jim got not only a loyal employee but also hot tamales. Ruth's mother, Shelby Bowers, makes them once a week, just like she does for dinners at the Hudson Grove Gospel Church in Farragut. Encased in tamale paper, they are filled with a mixture of beef and country sausage. One customer orders four dozen to ship to her son overseas. The shipping cost alone exceeds $200, for tamales priced at $14 a dozen.

Covered in Ruth's chili, those tamales become a Full House. Some say the combination is a Knoxville invention.

The chicken salad, tuna salad, egg salad, and pimento cheese at Long's are all house-made. The pimento cheese is a classic mid-twentieth-century lunch counter combination of mayonnaise, pimentos, salt, and pepper, added to cheese freshly grated from a five-pound block.

I ask Hank to point out a family favorite on the menu, and he directs me to a platter-sized slab of thick-cut Clifty Farms country ham with a side of cheese eggs.

"We put bacon on everything," Ruth adds. "On the Long's Burger, on tuna salad, egg salad. We were adding bacon long before the fast-food places started doing it."

On a weekday, Long's goes through about twenty pounds of bacon. On Saturdays, that quantity jumps to forty and even fifty pounds.

Underscoring the hearty nature of the food at Long's, Ruth Pate claims, "I don't make regular-size pancakes."

Sometimes six milkshake machines whir at once. In addition to the photographs on the walls that tell the history of

*A slab of Tennessee country ham and a helping of cheese eggs at Long's. Photo by Fred Sauceman.*

University of Tennessee athletics, the menu acknowledges the presence of the university as well. The Big Orange Milkshake, Hank says, is "like an Orange Julius, with ice cream and orange juice."

Long's has employed hundreds of UT students over the years, at the fountain and in the pharmacy. "The student employees are always upbeat when people aren't feeling well," Hank says. "For the athletes who eat here, it's good for them to break away for a while and be a part of the community."

In 2006, Long's celebrated its fiftieth anniversary for an entire week. A different radio station held a remote broadcast every day of the week.

Amid all the constants at Long's over the years are the Christmas murals painted by Gail Hinton on the storefront windows. At the same time, with increased competition and outlets, semi trucks no longer pull up to the back door and unload stacks of Russell Stover candy.

Still, this family-owned pharmacy and fountain has kept the best of the old, that feeling of family and community connection.

"My dad raised half this county," Hank says proudly.

"I love it here," Ruth adds. "It's always been like family. There's nothing they wouldn't do for me."

Whether in search of cough medicine or chicken salad, Long's loyal customers feel the same way.

*Long's Drug Store*
*4604 Kingston Pike*
*Knoxville TN*
*865-588-9218*

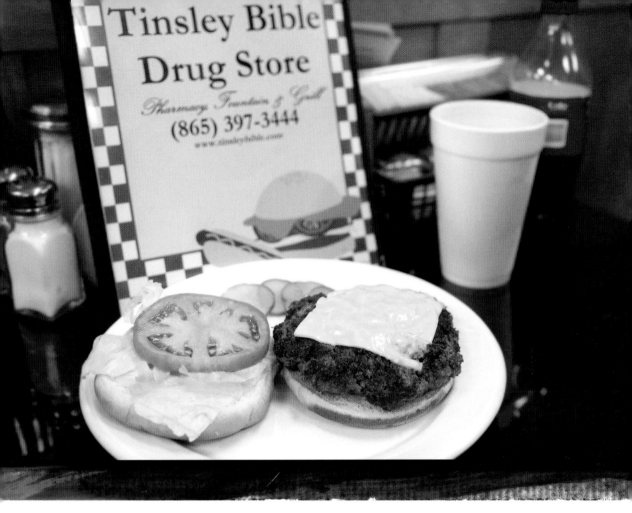

# THE BIBLE BURGER CURE

**PEGGY FAIN WOULD SIT AT HER SEWING MACHINE ALL DAY,** looking at the clock. The constant pressures of her job at a hosiery mill in Dandridge, Tennessee, prevented her from talking much. She was miserable in a job that lasted thirty-two years. Staying quiet was not in Peggy's nature.

In 1991, though, things changed. Peggy heard of an opening at the Tinsley-Bible Drugstore in downtown Dandridge, and she landed the position. There, she was not just allowed to talk; she was encouraged to.

"'Talk' is my middle name," says Peggy. "I was so happy to be able to talk, to make up for all those years."

*The Bible Burger memorializes a Tennessee pharmacist. Photo by Larry Smith.*

*Tinsley-Bible has operated at the same location in Dandridge since 1911. Photo by Larry Smith.*

She has never lived more than about seven miles from Tennessee's second oldest town, on the banks of the French Broad River. All her life she has been a customer of the drugstore, a business that opened in 1911.

If Peggy had a job description, it would be a complex one. She's a hostess, a public relations representative, a confidante, a counselor, a cook, a soda jerk, and more. In short, it's Peggy's job to make sure customers slow down and appreciate this piece of the American past.

Bob Jarnagin is Jefferson County's official historian. He has been a customer at Tinsley-Bible since he was a boy, when he rode his bicycle a mile into town to play the pinball machine. Bob now runs the insurance agency his grandfather started in Dandridge in 1920.

"The soda fountain drugstore is a dying breed, so I love to show this one off," says Bob, who arrives around four o'clock every other day from his office just around the corner for a double chocolate milkshake at Tinsley-Bible. "This place has the feel of a time gone by."

Ask Bob about Jefferson County history and his countenance lights up. "After clearing land and building cabins, the people who settled this area went to work immediately to build schools and churches," Bob relates. "They were a tough breed. They settled America's first wild west, which is what I consider East Tennessee to be.

"I also think it tells us something about the caliber of these people that they picked a woman, in January of 1793, to name their town for. They honored the first First Lady of our country, Martha Dandridge Custis Washington, from Virginia."

Fishing, tourism, and interest in American history bring folks to Dandridge. And so does the Bible Burger.

Concocting a scriptural connection might make a better story, but Jefferson Countians, sticklers for historical accuracy, point out that the burger is simply a way to memorialize a man. Dr. P. A. Tinsley, who opened the drugstore, was a medical doctor. He hired his nephew, Walter "Prock" Tinsley, to be the druggist. When Walter died in 1933, Dr.

Tinsley hired Lloyd "Doc" Bible, a newly minted pharmacy school graduate from the University of Tennessee in Memphis.

When pharmacist Don Rose bought the business in 1986, he wisely kept the name of the drugstore and the name of its heralded hamburger.

"I'm proud of Don Rose for keeping the historic character of this building," says Bob Jarnagin. "People come from far and wide to get a real hamburger made with real ground beef, not one of these frozen patties."

Peggy Fain says when the car show comes to town, she'll holler out the front door of the drugstore, "Come on in and get your Bible Burger. It's holy cow."

Whereas most slaw in East Tennessee is bound with mayonnaise, the slaw that tops a Tinsley-Bible hot dog is mustard based.

Drugstore manager Lynn Hixson says some diners compare the slaw's flavor to potato salad. "I would say it's more like a fresh relish," he adds.

"We had one lady, her daughter was pregnant and lived in North Carolina, she'd get hot dogs, put the slaw in a Tupperware bowl, put it on ice, and take all that home to her daughter," Peggy recalls. "She still hardly ever gets less than a dozen hot dogs."

The year 1993 marked another bit of history at Tinsley-Bible. It was the advent of soup beans and cornbread.

"Don, the owner, was real sick, in the hospital," Peggy remembers. "When I went to the hospital, he asked me for soup beans and cornbread. We added them to the menu, and I fry the cornbread on the grill."

While feeding Dandridge, Tinsley-Bible remains a full-service drugstore. "We fill prescriptions, do immunizations, handle prescriptions for assisted-living facilities," says Lynn Hixson. "Everything you do at a chain drugstore you can do here."

And, of course, a whole lot more.

"People from out of state write me and call me," says Peggy. "It's wonderful to know there are such good people in the world. From not being able to talk, I've gone to: 'Hey, how are you? Where are you from? Where did you live before then?' I put them through the drill."

Maybe there is something divine about that hamburger after all.

Tinsley-Bible
Drugstore
1224 Gay Street
Dandridge TN
865-397-3444

## HORNET DOGS AT TUCKAHOE

**ROGER BAULT DOES ROADWORK ALL OVER KNOX COUNTY, TENNESSEE.** But at lunchtime, road repair somehow always leads him to 8908 Kodak Road. His destination is the Tuckahoe Trading Post, a building dating to somewhere between 1914 and 1917.

The Thursday pork chops, he says, are "so tender you don't have to have a knife."

Given his job with the highway department, Roger knows virtually every road in the area. He thinks the Tuckahoe Trading Post is the only old country store of its kind still left in the county.

My introduction to Tuckahoe was the chance to go on a milk delivery with Colleen Cruze from Cruze Dairy, just about two miles down the road. Tuckahoe's co-owner Kim Worley says folks drive from Powell, Dandridge—twenty or thirty miles—to buy Cruze milk and buttermilk.

I walk to the back of the store and find Kim with a black-iron skillet in hand. She has already covered the bottom with butter and brown sugar

*The Tuckahoe General Store was built around the time of World War I. Photo by Larry Smith.*

and is layering in rings of pineapple, the beginnings of a pineapple upside-down cake.

Tuckahoe has been a restaurant for about thirty years. Breakfast there means fresh brown gravy, made with sausage from Swaggerty's, another neighboring company in Kodak, Tennessee. That gravy, with a bacon-grease base, is black-iron skillet cooking, too. It's served over scratch-made biscuits.

Just as the store links back to another era, so do its prices. The Hornet Dog takes its name from Kim's son Brandon's middle-school team mascot. Its price, eighty-eight cents, reflects his jersey number. Brandon is now in college, but the price has never changed for a hot dog dressed with chili, cheese, and jalapeño peppers.

"Everybody around here is related one way or other," says Kim. "When kids grow up, they try to find places around here to live. Everybody who works here is family. It's a home-style atmosphere. We know everybody who comes in. If we don't, we investigate until we do."

Like many rural stores in the South, this one was once paired with a mill. Its product was Belle of Tuckahoe flour.

Kim and her mother, Sandy Maples, understand the role of the country store as community gathering place. Before Christmas, they bring in a photographer who takes free pictures of children with Santa Claus. Those pictures are displayed under glass on the old counter all year long.

It's a simple way to make sure new generations never forget what it means to appreciate a place.

*Pineapple upside-down cake in a black iron skillet is a Tuckahoe trademark. Photo by Larry Smith.*

The Tuckahoe Trading Post
8908 Kodak Road
Knoxville TN
865-933-4939

*Zack Brine is the college-educated meat-cutter at Ye Olde Steak House. Photo by Fred Sauceman.*

# BIG STEAKS AND BIG ORANGE

**"IF I HAD TO ATTRIBUTE OUR SUCCESS TO ANY ONE THING,** it would be the University of Tennessee." That's the opinion of Cheryl Wilson, shared by her sister Nancy Ayres and their brother David King. They run Ye Olde Steak House, which their father Bunt King and mother Helen opened on Chapman Highway in Knoxville, Tennessee, in 1968.

On Friday nights before UT football games, it's not unusual for some 800 people to eat there. With tailgating being so popular on football Saturdays, the biggest crowds of the weekend show up on Fridays.

"Years ago, when kickoff was always at two o'clock, the women would come in here wearing wool suits with mums pinned on them, to eat dinner after they had sat out in the sun all afternoon," remembers Cheryl.

Ye Olde Steak House remains a favorite of former UT quarterback Peyton Manning and his family. There's a photographic shrine to the Mannings on the wall of the restaurant.

"When he comes in, kids line up for autographs," says Nancy. "He signs every one of them without fail."

BUTTERMILK &
BIBLE BURGERS

Former Volunteer coach Johnny Majors is a regular, bringing children and grandchildren for birthdays.

Ye Olde Steak House has even earned the affection of opposing coaches. On the wall is a letter from the late Ralph "Shug" Jordan, dated July 1, 1975, his last year as head football coach at Auburn University.

"You can rest assured when I return to Knoxville, and I am sure that I will since our son is living in Norris, that I will look forward to enjoying the warmth and great food at your lovely establishment once again," Jordan wrote.

The reputation of Ye Olde Steak House has always rested with Iowa beef, char grilled. The restaurant has employed a couple of the same cooks for forty years. Zack Brine, one of the younger ones, started working there when he was a sophomore at South-Doyle High School. He has graduated from busing tables to grilling steaks, earning, along the way, degrees from Pellissippi State Community College and Tusculum College.

"Cooking steaks here is a three-part system," Zack says. "First we put the meat on the grill and mark it up, then it goes to a gigantic cast-iron skillet in vegetable oil, then back on the grill. Steaks are served in a seasoned butter."

Those steaks caught the attention of former Penn State quarterback Todd Blackledge, who featured the restaurant in his "Taste of the Town" series on ESPN. Blackledge's favorite steak is the twenty-ounce strip, with sides of broccoli casserole and Woodshed Potatoes.

"After that aired, people were calling in from all over the country asking us how to make Woodshed Potatoes and broccoli casserole," says Nancy.

*The sides that ESPN viewers craved: broccoli casserole and Woodshed Potatoes. Photo by Fred Sauceman.*

The potatoes originated in Bunt King's home kitchen. They are rounds of fried potatoes, with the skin on, cooked with onions and seasoned liberally with black pepper, a common East Tennessee repast.

The blue cheese dressing at the steak house was once country club fare. Bunt King paid a cook ten dollars for the recipe at Holston Hills Country Club.

Another Bunt King idea was carving fortune-cookie-like sayings into the backs

of chairs. "The generous soul will be made rich," reads one. "Life is a great bundle of little things," says another.

One of those "little things" at Ye Olde is the use of tongue depressors to serve cheese spread, an appetizer that always appears on the table. Those tiny utensils scoop out about 200 pounds of cheese spread every week.

While some restaurants restrict prime rib to weekends, it's an everyday offering at Ye Olde Steak House, slow roasted all day, beginning at ten o'clock in the morning.

One of the many celebrities who have visited the restaurant is actress Margot Kidder, who announced upon arrival that she didn't eat meat and then admitted upon departure that the prime rib was the best she'd ever had.

Around 1970, char-grilled shrimp was added to the menu. Among the desserts is red velvet cake—further support for my contention that Knoxville, Tennessee, leads the world in per capita consumption of this red-dyed chocolate cake.

Cheryl and Nancy tell me that customers often come across old gift certificates from the restaurant, dating back to the 1970s. Consistent with their customer-first philosophy, they always honor such certificates.

Bunt King died in 1987 and Helen in 2003. At no time, though, did the family consider closing, even when a fire forced them to relocate downtown to the L & N station while the Chapman Highway structure was being rebuilt.

Cheryl, Nancy, and David memorialize their parents through a superior product and hard work, whether it's fielding constant phone calls, cutting meat, or hosting famous football stars. They've kept much of their parents' influence throughout the restaurant—
the most important being their father's clever slogan, "Food Fit for a King."

Ye Olde Steak House
6838 Chapman Highway
Knoxville TN
865-577-9328

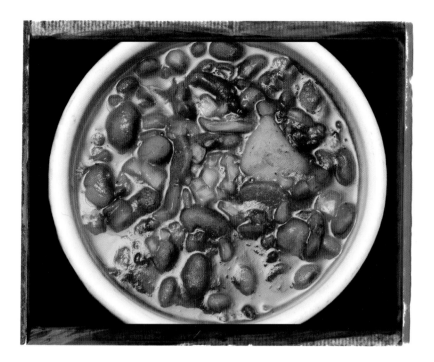

# PINTOS AND PERSISTENCE

**"WE MAKE BEANS ALL THE WAY.** We start off with a little bit of beef broth from our beef stew in the bottom of the bowl, a small potato, the beans, and then the onions on top, and we have Beans All the Way."

That's Donna Hartsell's description of the soup beans that have been served since the 1950s at what is now The Bean Barn.

Romie and Zella Mae Britt opened Britt's Grill on Depot Street in downtown Greeneville, Tennessee, beneath Waddell Hardware, in 1946. Romie Britt was born in Glasgow, Kentucky. He had a third-grade education. Zella Mae, born in Greene County, Tennessee, finished fifth grade. Together they built a business in beans.

In 1952, Romie and Zella Mae took over the Andrew Johnson Service Station on Summer Street, near the town's black community, and stayed there seventeen years. In this filling station and diner named for the seventeenth President of the United States, Romie and Zella Mae introduced Beans All the Way. They combined two dishes that had been simmering on Appalachian stoves for generations: soup beans and beef stew.

In 1969, Romie and Zella Mae moved the business to its current location on East Church Street, in a building that once housed Stills Grocery.

Zella Mae died in 1999. Romie died in 2003. Through marriage, the business is still in the family. Donna and her husband Jerry took over in December 1981.

"Well, I've brought people from all over the world to the Bean Barn, and if we're going to have one meal, I'm going to have it from here," says local philanthropist Scott M. Niswonger, founder of Landair Transport. "As you know, I have a restaurant downtown at the hotel, but this is the place they need to see to get a feel for what East Tennessee is all about."

Dan Walker, Greene County Trustee, says his father, Reagan Walker, came up with the recipe for Beans All the Way. Lard-seasoned, onion-sprinkled soup beans are common in the hills and valleys of East Tennessee. It's the beef stew that sets Beans All the Way apart.

Donna describes the recipe-less technique: "For my beef stew, I get a pressure cooker, put two large cans of tomatoes in it, get my hands down in there, squish the tomatoes up, salt and pepper, Kitchen Bouquet to add flavor and coloring, onions, and then I put the meat in, which Jerry takes care of, cuts it up himself, gets all the fat off of it—we put that in there, put the lid on it, cook it. The potatoes and carrots are cooked separately, and after the stew meat is done, we add that to the potatoes and carrots after they've cooked. I don't think I could write it down if I had to. It adds just a little bit of kick to the beans.

"I'm from South Carolina, and I sure didn't grow up eating soup beans. We ate butter beans and rice. That was one of my dad's favorite dishes, the butter beans over the rice, so I'm not used to being around soup beans until I moved to Tennessee."

Jerry cooks about ten pounds of beans at a time—usually two big pots every three days.

"All the pots we use are the pots that were here when I first took over. I don't usually go into buying too many new things," he says.

Romie and Zella Mae Britt were teenagers in 1929 when the stock market crashed. They knew hard times, and as a result, they could make a little food go a long way.

"Everybody always laughed at their beans and everything," recalls daughter Geraldine Pierce. "One man would always tell him, 'All I want is your profit, I don't want any of your beans in there, I just want the soup. I just want your profit.' Because you always had to pour extra water in it when they would cook down. They said, 'There goes Romie, putting more profit in those beans.'"

Although Romie and Zella Mae raised their children on soup beans, the siblings disagree to this day about how to serve them with cornbread.

"I don't know what the thing is about people crumbling their cornbread in their beans," says Geraldine. "You know, I've got a husband that does that. And I still don't really like them that way."

In a front-porch discussion on the subject, Geraldine's sister Janie Melton takes issue immediately.

"Now I like it that way. It soaks up the juice. You get more juice and beans at the same time—and the cornbread—and the onions has got to go in there, too."

The sisters do agree on one thing, though. Their father knew how to run a restaurant.

"Daddy always had an A grade on his food," remembers Janie. "And Daddy would know when they come in the door—he'd have their food sitting in their place because they eat the same thing every day."

Like many cooks of her generation, Zella Mae stretched her hamburger meat with bread. Dan Walker says a customer came in one day and asked what was on the menu. He initially declined on the hamburger choice, saying ground meat was hard on his stomach. Dan said his father Reagan told the customer, "There's not enough meat in those hamburgers to hurt you."

"Yeah, they used to laugh at Mom, she could take five pounds of hamburger meat and make ten pounds out of it," Janie adds. "And somebody would say they got food poisoning on that hamburger, and Reagan'd say, 'Not that hamburger you didn't. Not enough meat in it to make you have food poisoning.'"

Colorful customers have always been a part of life at Britt's Grill and The Bean Barn, including the late Fred Roberts, who said, "Well, used to I didn't come in here at all because I thought all they did was serve beans, and I don't do beans. Dr. Henard told me they'd kill me if I eat any more of them, so I quit eating them. But after I found out they served a real good breakfast, that's where I landed."

LeAnne Thwing, daughter of longtime Greeneville radio personality LeRoy Moon, picks up on the good breakfast theme.

"I like to eat biscuits and gravy. I am not kidding you, they are the best biscuits and gravy—besides my Nana's, God rest her soul—that I have ever eaten in my life. They are delicious, and my son feels the same way. We have come here—a group of our moms—every Wednesday morning. And the reason we come Wednesday morning is because we have several girls that work for doctors, and they're off on Wednesday. So we meet here on Wednesday mornings after we drop our children off and have breakfast. One of the husbands used to call us the Mini-Van Mafia. When you come in, you always know somebody that's here. You walk around to the tables before you get your food and talk to folks."

Scott Niswonger says it's the most egalitarian restaurant around. "You can be here at lunch with people that do all sorts of things—from making the houses to the Light and Power guys to painting the houses to guys that are trucking freight around the country."

Donna is proud of the cross-section of humanity that slows down for a bowl of Beans All the Way in this old grocery store building.

"We get kids, we get blue-collar workers, white-collar workers, senators, lawyers, doctors, factory workers— you name it, we get it."

Dress makes no difference, says Janie Melton. "You can come as you are at that restaurant, too. If you've been in the barn a-working, you can come in there and eat without changing clothes. Everybody's the same in there."

Donna, Jerry, and their staff are in constant motion, filling orders that stay lined up down the counter from seven o'clock breakfast through the ending of lunch at two o'clock, five days a week.

"It's a lot of hard work, but we've met a lot of great people over the years, a lot of great customers," Donna reflects. "We've seen kids grow up in this place and then bring their kids, and we've had a lot of loyal customers. We've shared family problems and family rewards with other people, and it's really been good that way."

Adds Scott Niswonger, "It's just a very unique place with a wonderful feel of Americana and small-town living. I wouldn't trade it for anything."

The Bean Barn
515 East Church Street
Greeneville TN
423-638-8329

BUTTERMILK &
BIBLE BURGERS

# REVIVAL AT OLD PILOT HILL

**AT THE OLD PILOT HILL GENERAL STORE, YOU DON'T CALL IN TO RESERVE A TABLE.** You call in to reserve ribs. Never a weekend passes without a rib sellout at this rejuvenated country store in the Philadelphia community of Washington County, Tennessee.

Like many a man in East Tennessee, George Walter fought for the Union during the Civil War. For his service, he was paid in land. His gov-

*The Old Pilot Hill General Store dates to 1902. Photo by Larry Smith.*

*The Sledge Cheeseburger.*
*Photo by Larry Smith.*

ernment grant consisted of some 320 acres. Layered with alluvial deposits from the nearby Nolichucky River, it was some of the richest land on the planet.

Walter paid William Hammer fifty dollars to build a store on the property. It was not only a center of commerce for the community but also served as a post office, and once a month a traveling magistrate would come by and convert the upstairs into a court-room.

Over the decades, as transportation improved and competition increased, the store fell into disrepair. Abandoned and slowly crumbling away, it was in need of a savior.

Donnie Hall and his wife Denise had grown tired of living in his native Florida. For four years, they had traveled around the country looking to buy a country store. A deal for one in Waxahachie, Texas, fell through. They found a few other stores, but they were too dilapidated. On a visit to East Tennessee to see an old high school friend of Donnie's, Denise picked up a real-estate book. In one of those "meant-to-be" moments, the book fell open to a photograph and a listing for a country store called Old Pilot Hill.

"There it was," recalls Denise. "The store was for sale. It had been on the market four years."

They decided to call the realtor that day, even though, as Donnie says, it was "a sad-looking little picture." The Halls closed the deal that very day.

In Florida, Donnie had owned a construction business. He put those skills to work saving the old store. Weeds had grown as high as the windows. The store's contents—scales, counter, pictures—had all been auctioned off, except for the shelves. The interior was painted baby blue.

Five months of scraping, cleaning, painting, and scavenging followed. The Halls purchased the old counter that had been used at the Western Auto Store on Depot Street in downtown Greeneville, Tennessee. They salvaged some display cases out of an old tobacco barn in Greene County. Denise cleaned out a Florida Ben Franklin store of thread, buttons, and cloth—all for sale now at the general store.

BUTTERMILK &
BIBLE BURGERS

The porch the Halls have added has become a gathering spot for the area's bluegrass musicians. "On Thursday nights they form a big circle and pick until nine or ten o'clock," says Donnie. "We have a full house. In fact, I tell people they'd better bring lawn chairs."

One idea Donnie initially resisted, says Denise, was the serving of food. He had a barbecue business in Florida, and when the subject of food at Old Pilot Hill came up, Denise warned him about the hard work and long hours.

Customers from all over who eat at the store are glad the Halls overcame the initial hesitation.

"The slower the better," Donnie says, speaking not only about life in the Philadelphia community but also about barbecue. "We use bone-in Boston butts for our pulled pork plates and sandwiches. Our ribs are baby back pork loin and very meaty. Our dry rub is Memphis-style, and our sauce has Memphis connections, too—sweet and tomato-based, with no vinegar.

*Donnie Hall is a firm believer in "low and slow" barbecue. Photo by Larry Smith.*

"I have a propane burner and put hickory wood on there to get it going. Then I turn the gas off and cook with the hickory wood." His ribs are so good they've even caused confrontations, when neophyte customers don't realize they have to be reserved ahead of time.

Reading the menu at Old Pilot Hill is a history lesson. The double-patty Sledge Cheeseburger with an onion ring on top is named after William Hammer, builder of the store. The Hammer Burger is a single patty. The Snapp Dog, an all-beef hot dog wrapped in bacon and deep-fried, echoes the name of the road where the store is located. The Mule Burger means fried bologna, a Southern Appalachian favorite, and the name was borrowed, with permission, from a store in the Rheatown community. The Riddle Griddle grilled cheese sandwich memorializes a former owner of Old Pilot Hill. A chicken sandwich pays homage to the Nolichucky River, less than a mile from the store.

"We wanted to incorporate this community into our menu and make it a little bit more fun," says Denise. "Out of anywhere we've been, nothing compares to the beauty here. We have the most beautiful view, and the people in this area live by the old way of treating people right."

121
BUTTERMILK &
BIBLE BURGERS

Old Pilot Hill
General Store
826 Snapp Bridge Road
Limestone TN
423-202-0289

During times when they are able to slow down, Donnie and Denise look across the Philadelphia Community Cemetery. George Walter, who died ten years after his store was built, is buried a short walk from the front porch. Looking toward the mountains, the Halls can see two tiny white churches, one a Cumberland Presbyterian and one a United Presbyterian, less than 100 yards away from each other, having split for political reasons.

"They must not have been too mad at each other," Donnie laughs. "They didn't go very far."

A few years after buying the store, the Halls were able to purchase the house next door, so they often don't leave the property for days at a time.

"What tugs at my heart and makes me feel good is seeing the people who live here in the community," Donnie says. "They come in here and eat. Maybe their neighbors down the road will come in, and they hadn't talked in a year. We love to see the neighbors getting back together and talking and being sociable again."

Old Pilot Hill has regained its place as the hub of the community, thanks to this enterprising couple from Florida.

"It's really rewarding when customers come in and are elated with the fact that their childhood memories are rejuvenated," says Denise. "You can always tell the people who come in the door who have been here before. They pause, and you can see they're looking for anything familiar from when they were a child. A lady came in here recently and said the last time she was in here was eighty-five years ago. She told me where everything was when she was a six-year-old child. To have people come in and share childhood memories like this is very rewarding."

## DINING IN THE KNOW

**IF YOU WANT TO KNOW WHAT'S HAPPENING IN ELIZABETHTON AND CARTER COUNTY,** Tennessee, there are WBEJ radio, the *Elizabethton Star* newspaper, and the City Market.

There are no secrets at the City Market. Secluded booths are nonexistent. A table tucked away in a quiet corner is not an option. You're within sight and earshot of everyone. Conversations cross from table to table. Opinions fly.

While some downtowns are dying, Elizabethton thrives, thanks to community gathering spots like the City Market. Owner Jennifer Hughes has kept the name that reveals the restaurant's past. Groceries were once sold there. And although it's primarily a restaurant now, you can still buy

*City Market regulars know to order dessert first. Photo by Fred Sauceman.*

seasonal produce at the City Market. Just inside the door, on my last visit, were baskets filled with sweet potatoes and apples.

Across from the produce is the dessert case. A City Market dining rule is to select your dessert when you walk in the door. Do so any later and you risk falling victim to a sellout. Jennifer's confections go fast.

Demand for banana split pie, coconut pie, chocolate pie, pumpkin pie tarts, Hershey bar cake, and Dreamsicle cake is high and constant. And, by the way, those aren't dessert choices spread over a month. Jennifer recently offered them all in one day.

The City Market is short-order splendor. It's a hamburger-hot dog place of the highest order, but at the same time, never a day passes without a simmering pot of soup beans and pans of house-made cornbread.

While the City Market is a know-all, hear-all kind of place, there is one closely guarded secret. Folks in Carter County know to skirt around it. You don't ask what Jennifer puts in her chicken salad. You just enjoy it. That chicken salad makes the rounds in the county. It's Jennifer's most-requested dish for catered events.

She will tell you, though, that her chicken salad "is homemade, with all white meat chicken, and is smoother than the chunky varieties. And we sell a ton of it," she adds.

Southern fried chicken salad is another menu mainstay at the City Market. No light salad with a few flecks of meat, it is instead covered in chunks of seasoned chicken.

A magazine editor once asked me to list and describe my top ten dining spots in Northeast Tennessee. That's always a dangerous proposition, and a difficult one, considering the variety of eateries in our region. But the City Market made the list. It's an E Street institution.

The City Market
449 East E Street
Elizabethton TN
423-543-1751

# A MARBLE MEMORIAL TO POP

**"HAFA ADAI."** In Chamorro, the native language of Guam, it's a greeting—a "Hello" or a "What's up?"

Those eight letters are affixed to the door of Pop Ellis Soda Shoppe and Grill in downtown Abingdon, Virginia. "Pop" Ellis was Harold Ross Ellis, who died in 2005 but whose name lives on at his son Doug's business on the town's Main Street. Hafa Adai may be a foreign phrase, but it's right at home in this Southwest Virginia setting.

Pop Ellis Soda Shoppe and Grill is an American success story. The themes are common in these Appalachian Mountains: patriotism, devotion to family, love of community, and service to others.

*Harold "Pop" Ellis. Photo courtesy Doug Ellis.*

Harold Ellis graduated from Elizabethton High School in Tennessee in 1942, shortly after America's entry into World War II. "And Dad couldn't get into the Marine Corps fast enough," says son Doug.

Harold was a witness to history on several fronts in the Pacific Theater of Operations. He was stationed on Guam with the 3rd Marine Division when the United States won the island back from Japan. His outfit was among the third wave of troops on Iwo Jima.

"He saw some of the nastiest fighting of the war," Doug says. "But he loved Guam. In the 1970s he returned there and fell in love with it all over again. That's why we have Hafa Adai on our door."

When Harold returned to East Tennessee after the war, his sister Marg met him at the bus station and told him she had enrolled him in college at East Tennessee State. (Their mother had died when Harold was twelve.)

Marg knew her brother's dream was to become a pharmacist. While in high school, he had dipped ice cream and worked as a soda jerk at City Drug in Elizabethton. After completing his studies at East Tennessee State, he went on to finish pharmacy school at the University of Tennessee in Memphis in 1949.

After jobs in Johnson City and Mountain City, Harold was recruited by the West End Pharmacy in Abingdon, Virginia, in 1951. He spent the remainder of his career in Abingdon.

"The community embraced him," says Doug.

When Harold opened his own place, Ellis Pharmacy, in 1954, banker Fred Buck loaned him money, and in the discussion about a payment plan, all Buck would say was, "I won't let you starve."

In 1959, when Harold built the building that now houses Pop Ellis Soda Shoppe and Grill, he was criticized for not having a soda fountain. "Those things are on the way out," he would say.

Harold was among the first pharmacy owners to create a drive-through window, what his son calls "forward thinking for the time."

Never in Harold's lifetime did he operate a soda fountain, but he acquired one in 1976 when he bought out Peoples Drug Store. That marble fountain sat in the Ellis basement for over thirty years.

Ellis Pharmacy eventually ran its course as a drugstore. Harold died in 2005. Two years later, Doug and his mother Yvonne sold the drugstore to Rite-Aid, one of some fourteen pharmacies in Abingdon. The last day of operation for the Ellis Pharmacy was May 15, 2007. On May 16, 2008,

Pop Ellis Soda Shoppe and Grill opened, named for Harold, the man who had never sold a sundae.

Doug describes the menu as "upper end sandwiches and salads." When Harold was being treated for lung cancer at the University of Virginia Hospital in Charlottesville, Doug would eat Gus Burgers at the White Spot. In developing the menu for Pop Ellis, Doug decided that this University of Virginia student favorite, a cheeseburger with a fried egg on top, would work well in Abingdon, too.

Pop Ellis also serves a hot dog topped with pimento cheese, which is then run under a broiler. "You have to eat it with a knife," Doug advises.

"People brag about our milkshakes as much as anything on the menu," Doug adds. "A lot of places use a mix and milkshake ice cream. We don't. We use premium ice cream, eighteen to twenty percent butterfat—and the milkshakes are twenty ounces, at least. We bring you a glass, and you spoon from the cup into the glass. That's old school."

One day in September 2008, Doug and his staff started noticing a police presence in the intersections of downtown Abingdon beginning about two o'clock in the afternoon.

"Then I saw two 'suits' walk around our building," Doug recalls. "I asked what was going on. The man was not rude, but he didn't answer. Twenty minutes later, the same man asked for the owner, saying that Senator Barack Obama would like to have an impromptu visit and meal."

It turns out that another celebrity was already there: Big Daddy Don Garlits, the king of drag-racing. Garlits had run for Congress in Florida and lost on the Republican ticket.

"This was mass chaos for us," Doug remembers. "We made about twenty-five milkshakes before Mr. Obama arrived, so that he could treat the press corps."

*This marble fountain was stored in the Ellis basement for over 30 years. Doug Ellis says the milkshakes served on it now are "old school." Photo by Fred Sauceman.*

127

BUTTERMILK &
BIBLE BURGERS

What did the future president of the United States order at Pop Ellis Soda Shoppe and Grill? A Pop's All-American Cheeseburger, sweet potato fries, and a vanilla milkshake.

"He and I talked about health care for fifteen minutes, especially the importance of home care," says Doug. "It was pretty special. CNN carried the visit live. Obama was in the area for a town hall meeting in Lebanon, coal country. Still today, people ask where he sat and get their picture made there."

The restaurant is filled with items from the Ellis family's extensive collection of pharmaceutical memorabilia. Visitors come in from all over the world, drawn to Abingdon by the Creeper Trail and the Barter Theatre, the State Theatre of Virginia.

"Most of all," Doug concludes, "I want them to appreciate the fact that this is a museum honoring old downtown drugstores and a memorial to my dad."

## MINERS AND MEATBALLS

**I HOLD A DEEP RESPECT FOR RESTAURANTS THAT HAVE NEVER FORGOTTEN THEIR FOUNDERS.**
Enter Minard's Spaghetti Inn, located in Clarksburg, West Virginia, and you immediately see a shrine. It memorializes Rose and Michael Minard. Their portraits are framed in gold, right inside the front door.

In 1937, Rose started feeding glassworkers right out of the kitchen. At first, most of her dining guests were Italians. The Italian population in this part of West Virginia is significant. Many of those immigrant families were attracted to the area because of the opportunities it afforded to work in glass factories and coal mines.

"In this area, they also had a railroad system that was active during the wars," says Rose's grandson, Mike Minard, who runs the family restaurant today. "And she wanted to start feeding the guys coming off work late."

The resourceful Rose plated up her spaghetti, meatballs, and lasagna on the family dining room table. That table still holds a heralded place right up front inside the Minard's of today.

129
BUTTERMILK &
BIBLE BURGERS

*The sign says it all: tradition. Photo by Fred Sauceman.*

*Minard's had its origin at the family dining table. Photo by Fred Sauceman.*

"A lot of the southern Italians that came through Ellis Island settled in this part of West Virginia," Mike tells me. "Our food has always reflected that, with heavier, meatier red sauces. Our original sauce recipe has never changed."

A popular dish today at Minard's is Pasta Suprema: freshly ground Italian sausage, diced portobello mushrooms, peppers, and marinara sauce served over spaghetti.

Still today, the Minard family reserves three entire days every year to do nothing but can their own peppers, usually around 100 cases.

"And that gets us through the year," says Mike. "They're sweet, with a little hot, to give a medium flavor. It's a tradition we're really proud of."

The Minard's Spaghetti Inn kitchen has been a training ground for several restaurant cooks who have gone on to establish their own businesses in the Clarksburg and Fairmont area. "We all go to each other's restaurants," Mike says. "Most of us are related. We have pictures of the owners of other restaurants in our kitchen working together."

Like many Italian families, the Minards dropped the ending vowel, the "i," from their last name so that they would not be viewed as different, as "foreign." The Brunett family, owners of Clarksburg's Tomaro's Bakery since 1914, did the same thing. Now, however, the city of Clarksburg proudly hosts a yearly West Virginia Italian Heritage Festival in late summer.

With over three quarters of a century of history behind it, Minard's Spaghetti Inn has never abandoned the spaghetti-and-meatball and lasagna dishes Rose first served around the family table to those glassworkers and miners during the years of the Great Depression.

BUTTERMILK &
BIBLE BURGERS

Minard's Spaghetti Inn
813 East Pike Street
Clarksburg WV
304-623-1711

# INSIDE MARIO'S FISHBOWL

**BARE WALL SPACE IS SCARCE AT MARIO'S FISHBOWL** in Morgantown, West Virginia. Handwritten notices cover almost every inch. A constant eating and drinking Olympics takes place here. Competitors document their records and post them for all to see. In 1968, for example, Gene Dragavich drank a large fishbowl of beer in four seconds. And Bruce Bellman consumed eighteen hot dogs in one hour on February 21, 1969.

Tom and Anna Torch opened the business as the Richwood Avenue Confectionary in 1950. Later they started serving beer in large goblets. The glass vessels were products of the flourishing glass industry in West Virginia. When Rose and Mario Spina took over in 1963, they began calling the goblets "fishbowls."

"There are lots of records about how fast you can drink a fishbowl," says Bill Cain, a native of Morgantown and a graduate of Morgantown High School and West Virginia University. Now a school administrator in eastern Maryland, the former basketball coach often makes the pilgrimage back to the Fishbowl.

"Sitting right here one day, my buddy, who just got back from the military, from boot camp, said, 'I'll bet you five bucks I can eat this glass.' I said, 'It's not worth five bucks for me to see you eat the glass.' He said, 'You pay for the glass; I'll eat a chunk out of it.' He ate a chunk of glass, not out of one of these fishbowls but out of a Pilsener glass, and swallowed it. At that time I was working night shift at the hospital, and they told me that's the best way I know to die, to die from hemorrhaging.

"Where you're sitting right now used to be a magazine rack, and we'd come and read comics and drink sodas. I'm sixty-two years old, and I knew it when I was five or six years old. It was a place to hang out. It was a place to sit down and have a beer and reminisce, remember. I was down here all the time, all the time. We used to get the hot dogs here, the chili dogs. The food's always good. I know a lot of stories about West Virginia athletics were resolved here on who should they hire, who they shouldn't hire."

Karen and Mark Furfari bought Mario's Fishbowl in 1997. Karen says that, despite all the drinking records, it's a family-oriented business.

"We have customers who, when they have a newborn and they're discharged from the hospital, the first place they come with their newborn is the Fishbowl to have their picture taken with their baby in front of a fishbowl. Our clientele is a mixed bag: twenty-one-year-olds, twenty-two-year-olds, med students, law students, professionals. Mario's Fishbowl is very much an alumni hotspot. Football games, this is where the alumni want to come, whether they're in their seventies, their forties, their fifties, their thirties, it doesn't matter."

Karen, a former management consultant from St. Louis, patterns many of her current business practices after the ways of Mario and Rose Spina. Posted prominently inside Mario's Fishbowl still today, above bags of salted cashews, is a rectangle of brown paper, hand-lettered by Mario and Rose, in all capital letters. Written in green magic marker, it reads, "Your life is God's gift to you. What you do with your life is your gift to him, so take good care of it and drive careful because he cares. Have a good day. Love always, Mario and Rose." Karen says Mario and Rose looked after their customers almost like parents would.

"Mario always said that Rose was the boss. And Mario was a very kind man. He was quiet, he was very wise, and he was very committed to his customers and his customers' safety. Mario would take their ID when they came in the door and ordered a beer, and he would check their ID even if they were fifty years old. It didn't matter. He was taking your ID. And then he would file your ID in a magazine and he would say to you, 'You're on page forty-seven.' He basically held the ID as ransom for his glass. If you said to Mario, 'I can't remember that, Mario,' he would give you a pen and tell you to write the page number on your hand. And you couldn't leave until you were finished and approached Mario and got your ID, and then you were able to leave."

WVU alumna Sandy Maguran remembers another Mario Spina trademark: "We always tried not to look at Mario's hand where his big toe was grafted on to replace his lost thumb."

Customers could not, independently, post eating and drinking records on the wall. Mario and Rose had exacting standards. You had to earn your record, your bit of precious wall space.

"We do have a stopwatch, as Mario did, and we struggle with so many people just coming in and saying, 'I want to get on the wall, give me a slip so that I can put a record on the wall,'" Karen says.

Going back to the days of the Spina family, many of those records are written on the backs of cut-up cigarette cartons. No matter the material, though, each one had to be signed. To read them all would take hours. Karen shows me one, timed with that stopwatch to hundredths of a second: Herb Hand, extra large fishbowl, 5.98 seconds, February 24, 2007.

The capacity of a fishbowl goblet at Mario's would be easy to measure in fluid ounces, but "How much beer does a fishbowl hold?" is a question you never ask. Karen and her husband made a verbal commitment to Mario and Rose never to share that "secret." And to this day, Karen adds, "On occasion, we make people unhappy when we refuse to answer that question, and we have never answered that question."

Ben Kocker posted a claim that he did a shot of Tabasco in 1.26 seconds on February 12, 1999. "What a man," he declared. Below his message for the ages, a friend added the humbling footnote, "Puked."

BUTTERMILK &
BIBLE BURGERS

Fishbowl patron Leslie Filben Garrett recalls a customer who, after drinking several pitchers of beer, would balance a table on his chin.

"After the staff wildly applauded his feat, he was thrown out," Leslie says. "This was a weekly ritual, every Thursday night."

Customers at Mario's don't just compete to set beer-drinking and hot-dog-eating records. They eat cardboard coasters—the kinds made by beer distributors to promote their products.

"People have different methods for eating coasters," says Nikki Emerick, a server at the Fishbowl. "When we did the coaster-eating contest for the anniversary party that we have every year, there were people lined up along the bar. Some people tore the coaster into little pieces and put them right in their mouth. Other people soaked coasters in beer. I had a guy tell me that he thought the easiest way was to take it like a pill—tear it up into little pieces and then put it in your mouth and swallow it, with a drink. So that's what I've seen."

I ask Nikki if she's a coaster eater. "No, I'm not a fan of eating coasters, but I support it," she answers diplomatically.

Conventional, nourishing eating is perfectly acceptable at Mario's, too.

"We serve Philly cheesesteaks, chicken cheddar cheese-steaks," says Karen. "We have a fantastic Reuben. Our French fries are not frozen. We take potatoes and we hand-cut them. We have fishbowl chips which are hand-cut potato chips. Pretty much everything that we do here is made from scratch. Our meats and cheeses all come from Pennsylvania Macaroni Company in the Strip District in Pittsburgh."

Through the legacy of Mario and Rose Spina, whose photograph hangs prominently above the bar, the Fishbowl is testament to the influence of Italian immigrants in northern West Virginia. The goblet, the fishbowl itself, is a reminder of the role that glassmaking has played in the economy of the Mountain State. For Mark and Karen Furfari, it's important to remember that history.

"The rewarding part about owning Mario's Fishbowl is customers leave so happy," Karen tells me. "People you don't even know will approach you and say, 'Thank you so much, the food was great. Loved the atmosphere, the beer's fantastic, thank you so much for not changing Mario's Fishbowl.'"

*Mario's Fishbowl*
*704 Richwood Avenue*
*Morgantown WV*
*304-292-2511*

# GRAVY DAY

**IN WAYNESBORO, VIRGINIA,** Evelyn Dean, a hairdresser, and her husband Butch, a welder, decided to apply their manual dexterity to the kitchen and opened the Basic City Luncheonette in 1997. It gets its name from a section of Waynesboro. The Deans' welding business was located on the town's east side, and they say that finding a place to eat nearby used to be tough. So Evelyn and Butch took matters into their own able hands and exchanged curlers and torches for skillets and sinks at this restaurant near two busy railroad tracks and the post office.

Their daily specials quickly attracted diners from all over Augusta County and beyond. On Fridays, the lure is pork tenderloin and gravy, with a side of brown beans.

"We brown the pork and then take the leavings and make pan gravy," says Evelyn. "When we started out, we were frying thirty-five pieces of pork on Fridays. Now it's 400."

At lunchtime, that gravy is puddled into mashed potatoes. For breakfast, which is served all day, the seasoned, medium-brown gravy blankets biscuits or white bread.

After a dessert of what the Deans call The Cake—a mandarin orange creation with a pineapple-flavored icing—Evelyn says, "People stand out on the curb and watch the trains."

The Deans take pride in their hefty portions—enough, Evelyn says, "so that our older customers will have enough food for a second meal."

Basic City Luncheonette
408 North Commerce Avenue
Waynesboro VA
540-932-1790

# BRATWURST PIZZA AND FULL NELSONS

*The veggie pizza at Blue
Mountain Brewery,
Afton, Virginia. Photo
courtesy Tom Daly.*

**ITALY MEETS GERMANY AND THE PASTURE FIELDS OF VIRGINIA** on the welcoming
tables at Blue Mountain Brewery in Afton. Atop a crust of "half wheat
flour and half white flour" seasoned with honey and flavored with herbs, is
a scattering of bratwurst. The German-style sausage is produced nearby,
right in Nelson County, by Double H Farms. A topping of local apples
ties the pizza even closer to the central Virginia region. Bringing the pizza
full circle to its Italian past are caramelized sweet onions, mozzarella

cheese, and house-made marinara sauce, all finished with a reduction of balsamic vinegar.

"Bratwurst pizza is by far the most ordered and talked about item on our menu," says Mandi Smack, chief financial officer and marketing manager of Blue Mountain.

To accompany bratwurst pizza, many customers order a Full Nelson, Blue Mountain's copper-colored flagship Virginia pale ale. Virginia was once known as "the hop capital of the New World." For its ales and lagers, Blue Mountain cultivates its own hops and has established the state's first "hop cooperative" with Stan Driver of Hoot 'n' Holler Hops in Nellysford, also in Nelson County. Local hops are dried, vacuum-sealed, refrigerated, and used yearlong in each batch of Full Nelson.

A member of the Virginia Green Program, Blue Mountain engages in such conservation-minded practices as connecting rain barrels directly to its irrigation system at the hop farm.

Blue Mountain Brewery
9519 Critzer Shop Road
Afton VA
540-456-8020

## TWO TASTES OF OLD VIRGINIA

**THE YEAR 1940 WAS A DEFINING ONE FOR ROANOKE, VIRGINIA.** Amid the fear, dread, and uncertainty of World War II came the comfort of peanut soup.

Since its creation that year by Chef Fred Brown, peanut soup has fortified stomachs and souls in the Regency Room of the Hotel Roanoke. Its companion dish is one that has been served by Virginians for generations: spoonbread.

In 1994, writer Donlan Piedmont penned a history of the hotel. Those two dishes have defined the hotel so well over the years that Piedmont chose them for the title of his book: *Peanut Soup and Spoonbread*. In the book's preface, Marshall Fishwick, a professor at Virginia Tech, calls them "landmark dishes."

**BUTTERMILK &
BIBLE BURGERS**

*The Hotel Roanoke is known for its connection to the railroad, its ties to Virginia Tech, and its peanut soup and spoonbread. Photo by Fred Sauceman.*

The history of the hotel is closely intertwined with the railroad legacy of Roanoke. Norfolk and Western built the structure in 1882. The architectural style is Tudor Revival.

The property has gone through several changes of ownership over the years and is now operated by Virginia Tech. A wall of "Hokie Stone" marks the transition from the hotel to the adjoining conference center, managed by the City of Roanoke.

In fact, in order to arrange a calm and quiet night before home football games in Blacksburg, Virginia Tech's Coach Frank Beamer brings his players over for a Friday night stay.

Hotel Roanoke holiday buffets are legendary. Reservations must be made weeks if not months in advance. At Thanksgiving, the number of buffet reservations averages around 1,400. Two constants on those buffets are the peanut soup and spoonbread.

Until just a few years ago, the peanut soup recipe was a closely guarded secret. Despite its long culinary history, Chef Billie Raper says some diners are surprised to learn that soup can be made of peanuts.

Raper, a Richmond native, describes spoonbread as "a moist, soufflé-like version of cornbread."

After the edible history offered in the Regency Room, a walk through the hotel reveals links to Roanoke's past at every turn. In October 1935, Civil War veterans gathered on the lawn for a reunion. During World War II, military officers relaxed in the Pine Room.

Along Peacock Alley are photographs of Miss Virginia Pageant winners who have gone on to claim the title of Miss America. For many years, the Miss Virginia pageant was held in the hotel.

At Christmastime, more than twenty-five designer Christmas trees grace the building during the Fashions for Evergreens event.

Of the 331 guest rooms, not one is the same. Those rooms have survived fires, the Great Depression, and even closure. But now, with tea dances in the Crystal Ballroom and peanut soup on the menu every day, the Hotel Roanoke is in full glory.

The Hotel Roanoke
110 Shenandoah Avenue
Roanoke VA
540-985-5900

139

BUTTERMILK &
BIBLE BURGERS

# Hotel Roanoke Peanut Soup

| | | | | |
|---|---|---|---|---|
| 1/4 | pound butter | 1 | small onion, diced |
| 2 | stalks celery, diced | 3 | tablespoons flour |
| 2 | quarts chicken broth, heated | 1 | pint peanut butter |
| 1/3 | teaspoon celery salt | 1 | teaspoon salt |
| 1 | tablespoon lemon juice | 1/2 | cup ground peanuts |

*Peanut soup has been served at The Hotel Roanoke since 1940. Photo courtesy Hotel Roanoke.*

*Melt butter in cooking vessel and add onion and celery. Sauté for 5 minutes but don't brown.*

*Add flour and mix well. Add hot chicken broth and cook for 30 minutes.*

*Remove from stove, strain, and add peanut butter, celery salt, salt, and lemon juice. Sprinkle ground peanuts on soup just before serving. Serves 10.*

## PASTORING WITH PIE

**THE HUB IN ROCKY MOUNT, VIRGINIA, HAS HELD ON THROUGH SOME HARD TIMES.**
It opened in 1935, in the middle of the Great Depression, and still occupies the same spot on a hill above the railroad bridge. At one time, textile mills surrounded The Hub. Millworkers had a half hour for lunch, and they packed the place.

"Now all those textile mills are gone," says The Hub's owner, Richard Harrell. "One of the few industries left around here is Ply Gem, which makes windows just across the bridge from here."

In addition to The Hub's three-meal-a-day menu and about six gallons of sausage gravy served every Saturday, pie has kept the doors open. Richard says the pie recipes were salvaged from the long-defunct Rocky Mount Pastry Shop, where they originated in the 1920s and '30s.

*The Hub is a Depression-era business that held on. Photo by Fred Sauceman.*

For some reason, a cowboy adorns the cooler at The Hub. Photo by Fred Sauceman.

Butterscotch, chocolate, and coconut pies are made every day by Richard's wife Terry, who, as her husband says, "occasionally ventures out and makes others, like peanut butter crunch." The golden-orange color of her butterscotch pie is unforgettable.

Over its long history, The Hub has had only three owners. Butch and Mary Ann Wilcox ran the restaurant for thirty-six years and still can't stay away. "They'll come in and work every once in a while," says Richard.

He appreciates the help, since he splits his time between running The Hub and pastoring the 600-member Boones Mill Baptist Church just up the road.

His limestone-fronted restaurant with a cowboy painted on the outside cooler offers counter, booth, and table seating.

"Some of our local folks eat here two or three times a day," says Richard.

Pastoring a church and running a restaurant aren't all that different, he tells me. "You're just nourishing folks in different ways."

The Hub
245 North Main Street
Rocky Mount VA
540-483-9303

# FROM FARM TO TABLE IN FLOYD

**FLOYD COUNTY, VIRGINIA, CLAIMS MORE MUSICIANS PER CAPITA THAN NEW YORK CITY.** On The Crooked Road (Virginia's Heritage Music Trail) and within sight of the Blue Ridge Parkway sits Tuggles Gap Restaurant, where live music is performed every weekend.

Once the location of the Parkway Service Station, the pine-paneled restaurant near "the crest of the Blue Ridge" serves satisfying repasts, often with a southwestern touch and a vegetarian theme. Drawn by her "love of the rural environment," current owner Cheri Baker bought the restaurant and its accompanying twelve-room roadside motel two decades ago with her mother, Neil Baker. Risking their life savings, they moved cross-country from Grants, New Mexico, and brought with them recipes for making green and red chilies.

Those sauces are slathered over a beautiful breakfast burrito, stuffed with scrambled eggs, shredded cheese, tomato, and onion. The menu

BUTTERMILK &
BIBLE BURGERS

*Tuggles Gap sits near the Blue Ridge Parkway. Photo by Fred Sauceman.*

offers red "or" green chili, but Cheri says "and" is appropriate, too: red over one half and green over the other, a combination called "Christmas" in New Mexico. The red is the bolder of the two, made from an old New Mexico recipe using dried Anaheim peppers.

Tuggles Gap is fully aligned with Floyd County's long-standing farm-to-table focus. Hamburger meat is local, purchased at Slaughters' Supermarket in Floyd County. Vegetarian omelets are stuffed, whenever possible, with local squash, peppers, onions, and spinach—and, as Cheri says, "whatever is in the kitchen."

Tuggles Gap is a direct link to the early days of the Blue Ridge Parkway, when travelers along the thoroughfare began demanding quick access to lodging, food, and fuel. The original shell of the building that now houses Tuggles Gap Restaurant, about six miles outside the town of Floyd, dates to 1938.

*Left, the Tuggles Gap breakfast burrito has connections to New Mexico; right, Biscuits and gravy at Tuggles Gap. Photos by Fred Sauceman.*

BUTTERMILK &
BIBLE BURGERS

# THE JU-JU

**MY QUEST FOR ODDLY NAMED HAMBURGERS TOOK US TO THE DRY POND CAFÉ** in Patrick County, Virginia, near the North Carolina line, despite the best efforts of our GPS device to steer us into someone's driveway.

"GPSes don't work very good around here," says regular customer Patsy Oakley, who remembers when there actually was a pond at Dry Pond—a "swampy thing," she calls it, that eventually dried up.

The Dry Pond Café is a business without a sign. Nothing on Highway 103 says you're there. The restaurant's name is only painted on two windows.

*The Ju-Ju Burger memorializes Junior Lankford. Photo by Fred Sauceman.*

"It's a little brick building," owner Shvonda Cockram tells me over the phone as we plan our trip to Patrick County. "You'd think it was a house. It's a pretty big business considering how small it is and no sign."

Dry Pond Café is the home of the Ju-Ju Burger. Its name was a child's term of endearment.

Shvonda's parents owned the café from 1996 to 2010. "The kids my mama used to babysit called my dad, Junior Lankford, Ju-Ju," she says. "He died in 2005, and we've kept the name of the burger in his memory."

A Ju-Ju Burger is a bacon double cheeseburger—a half-pound of meat and two pieces of cheese.

While cooks at the Dry Pond Café construct Ju-Ju Burgers, they're also smashing baked potatoes with a wooden mallet and loading them with cheese, bacon, ham, grilled onions, peppers, and mushrooms.

Meanwhile, Bonnie Brown is making intensely colored sweet potato pie out of fresh sweet potatoes.

The Dry Pond Café is easy to overlook, but for travelers through this part of Virginia seeking good food and fellowship with local folks, it's a must stop.

The Dry Pond Café
2156 Dry Pond Highway,
near Stuart VA
276-694-6055

## ARCHITECTURE AT ODDS

**ON NORTH MAIN STREET IN HILLSVILLE, VIRGINIA,** two architectural styles couldn't be more different. The Hale-Wilkinson-Carter Home is a dominant downtown structure, adjacent to the Carroll County Courthouse. Built in 1845, the house, now with five stories and thirty-four rooms, became the home of multimillionaire George L. Carter, who made his fortune in coal mining and railroading. Carter died in 1936, ten years before another Hillsville landmark was set in place just a short walk down North Main.

*The architecture of the Hillsville Diner offers quite a contrast to the mansion up the street. Photo by Fred Sauceman.*

It's a prefabricated diner, constructed in Elizabeth, New Jersey, around 1940. By some accounts, the Jerry O'Mahony Diner Company built about 2,000 of them between 1917 and 1941. Only a few survive, including today's Hillsville Diner. Its first home, until 1946, was Mt. Airy, North Carolina. Then it was hauled to Hillsville, where it's been ever since. With its rounded metal ceiling and sliding front door, the diner has the feel of a streetcar. The hoods, the steam table, and the grill are all original.

And also from the 1940s, stewed beef holds on. Mac McPeak, third-generation owner of the Hillsville Diner, says it's not beef stew. "Stewed beef is simply cooked beef tips," he tells us, while covering half a platter with the historic dish, along with homemade cornbread muffins and "real" mashed potatoes. Mac isn't the first restaurant owner on our tour of places near the Blue Ridge Parkway to serve up mashed potatoes and place a heavy emphasis on the word "real."

In fact, it's an adjective that applies equally well to the Hillsville Diner itself and all it stands for as a symbol of small-town, Main Street America.

The Hillsville Diner
525 North Main Street
Hillsville VA
276-728-7681

BUTTERMILK &
BIBLE BURGERS

## "WE SMOKE, YOU SAUCE"

**BARBECUE HAS TRADITIONALLY BEEN RURAL FARE, BUT IN GALAX, VIRGINIA,** it's right downtown, on North Main Street. Since its opening in 2003, the Galax Smokehouse has been honored every year in a blind judging by the National Barbecue Association.

Dry-rub ribs smoked over hickory wood for four hours and pork butt for eleven are among the highlights of the extensive menu, which also features mesquite-smoked beef brisket covered in brown gravy. Owners Dan Milby and Ron Passmore tout hickory-smoked Idaho baking potatoes, mashed, loaded with cheese and sour cream, and baked.

149
BUTTERMILK &
BIBLE BURGERS

*Long known for fiddling, Galax, Virginia, is now gaining a reputation for barbecue. Photo by Fred Sauceman.*

The barbecue philosophy espoused by these two Florida natives is "we smoke, you sauce." The geography of their sauces is wide: a vinegary version with North Carolina connections; a tomato-based sauce that speaks of Tennessee; a spicy Texas blend; a mustard-infused sauce of South Carolina lineage; and a local addition called Susan's Sweet and Sassy, created by Rick Clark, the police chief in Galax, and named for his wife.

Running a barbecue joint represents a stark career change for both Dan and Ron, who once worked as "perfusion technicians," overseeing heart-lung machines during open-heart surgery procedures. Ron still works in health care, supervising all the EMS personnel in Grayson County while handling the finances of the Galax Smokehouse at night.

The Galax Smokehouse occupies the building that once housed Bolen's Drugstore, which opened in 1910. The drugstore's original counter and soda fountain remain.

Dan and Ron have transformed Galax into a barbecue hot spot. Around 12,000 people attend the Smoke on the Mountain Barbecue Championship, sanctioned by the Memphis in May organization, in mid-July every year.

Dan and Ron were once told that Virginia wasn't a barbecue state. They're doing their smoking best to dispel that myth.

The Galax Smokehouse
101 North Main Street
Galax VA
276-236-1000

# BIG BISCUITS AND BLUE DEVILS

**ONE MEASURE OF A RESTAURANT'S HOSPITALITY IS ITS SEATING.** The Campus Drive-In, located in Gate City, Virginia, offers counter stools, tables with chairs, and booths. And which one you choose depends on how full the place is, how much time you have on your hands, and how private you want your conversation to be.

The "culture" of The Campus is largely shaped by its location, adjacent to Gate City High School. To cast it as a twenty-first-century version of Arnold's from "Happy Days" would be to ignore the fact that customers eat there all their lives. Some even take three meals a day there.

BUTTERMILK &
BIBLE BURGERS

*Debra Dougherty
and Shirley Williams
serve breakfast at
The Campus. Photo by
Fred Sauceman.*

Biscuits and gravy served until noon have fueled Gate City Blue Devil linemen on their way to state championships in football, while grilled salmon satisfies restricted diets of retirees.

The term "family restaurant" is often overused in advertising, but at The Campus, it applies on two levels. Diners of all ages eat there, and the same family has continuously owned the restaurant since 1955. The late Darrel Dougherty opened it, and it's now overseen by his daughter-in-law Debra and her husband Allen.

A holdover from the days when Darrel ran Scott County's Taylor Theater is The Campus chili, simmered for hours. It's on the menu every day, as are soup beans, and some diners mix the two.

*Scratch-made biscuits and gravy, pork tenderloin, and eggs are among the breakfast selections at The Campus. Photo by Fred Sauceman.*

Debra says Campus patrons are pretty traditional in their tastes. "They like center-cut country ham and sandwiches on buns with lettuce and tomato."

Innovation has its place at The Campus, but not to the extreme. "What the hell's a croissant?" asked one customer a few years ago before

the French-style crescent roll was pulled from the menu.

Shirley Williams, a longtime Campus cook and server, did succeed in ramping up coleslaw. The innovation took hold and stayed. Debra says Shirley decided that "plain old coleslaw was not good enough with her fish," so she added cucumber, green bell pepper, tomatoes, and onion and started calling it slaw salad. Look for it with the fish special on Thursdays (not Fridays) and sometimes on Sundays.

Hand-patted jumbo hamburgers all the time, spaghetti with homemade meat sauce on Fridays, big hunks of meatloaf, and plates of country-fried steak with brown gravy are filling favorites at The Campus, along with strawberry milkshakes made with real berries and butterscotch pie capped with a mountain of meringue.

The menu at The Campus is not only full of food choices but also carries advertising, a holdover from the past that I've always liked. A drugstore, a heating and air-conditioning business, a funeral home, and the Virginia Farm Bureau all tout their services and products amid the listings of sirloin steak and cheese sandwiches and fried pork tenderloin with eggs.

Restaurants clearly have a role in building community pride, and there's no better example than this one, where respect for the traditions of Gate City High School sports is rivaled only by appreciation for scratch-made sausage gravy done right.

*Since 1955 The Campus Drive-In Has Fueled Footballers and Shaped a Community*

153

BUTTERMILK &
BIBLE BURGERS

The Campus Drive-In
432 Kane Street
Gate City VA
276-386-3702

## AWAITING CHICKEN DAY

**"IT'S FRIED CHICKEN AND DEVILED EGGS AND ICE TEA DURING THE DAY.** At night it's crab legs and ribeye steaks and beer."

That's how owner Teresa Smith Ray describes Harry's Place, a business started by her father in 1954 in a building built by her grandfather in the 1930s.

Harry's Place is the living room of Elkin, North Carolina. In a former pool hall, barber shop, and cab stand, diners sign their names on a clipboard and wait for tables—in the hallway, in the bar, outside. Conversation is constant.

"It's like coming home," Teresa says.

BUTTERMILK &
BIBLE BURGERS

*Harry's opened in 1954, in a building constructed in the 1930s. Photo by Fred Sauceman.*

The menu hasn't changed in three decades. At this neighborhood restaurant bordered by Elkin Creek and the railroad, Thursday is rarely called Thursday. It's chicken day. Split, bone-in breasts are pan-fried and accompanied by three vegetables, from a selection of about a dozen. Clara Darnell, an eighteen-year veteran of the Harry's Place kitchen, starts frying at four o'clock in the morning.

*The menu at Harry's hasn't changed in three decades. Photo by Fred Sauceman.*

Weekday customers are mainly local in this Surry County community where textiles once were king. On weekends, however, the town's push for tourism yields a largely out-of-town clientele, many on tours of Yadkin Valley wineries.

"There are about fifteen wineries within fifteen miles of Harry's," Teresa tells me.

Despite the changing face of the Yadkin Valley economy, though, Harry's Place means continuity and comfort.

Harry's Place
135 Front Street
Elkin NC
336-835-9693

BUTTERMILK &
BIBLE BURGERS

# A PORK CHOP CHAMP

**WITH TEN CHILDREN IN WALTER AND VIVIAN BROWN'S FAMILY,** not everyone could go to church. Someone had to stay home and cook. Usually that job fell to Doug Brown. "There was flour everywhere," says Doug, as he recalls cooking for his parents and nine brothers and sisters in Sparta, North Carolina.

Doug started in the restaurant business when he was sixteen. Now he and his wife Vera run Brown's Restaurant in downtown Sparta, and Doug is still slinging flour.

His most popular floured creation is pork chops. He spreads his hands about four feet wide to show me the size of the pork loins he uses. All the chops are hand-cut to make sure they're thick enough and stay juicy enough. The seasoning is light. The frying is quick. The result is profound.

"We had a man here who eventually ate 100 pork chops," Doug says. "He would let us know how many he was up to every time he came in."

In the Christmas-tree-growing county of Alleghany, hearty food is valued. Mashed potatoes, cooked apples, and pinto beans are on the Brown's Restaurant menu every day.

Saturday mornings bring a flurry of North Carolina liver mush orders. And, says Doug, "The kids love pancakes and French toast."

Members of the Brown family are constantly present at the restaurant: Doug, Vera, their sons Kydric and Fredrick. Air Force veteran David Evans serves as de facto host, busing tables, seating diners, and dispensing information about the gorgeous county of Alleghany.

"Twelve hours is a short day for me," Doug says. "Sometimes it's fifteen or sixteen. But I love seeing people enjoying their meal."

*Brown's Restaurant*
*115 Jones Street*
*Sparta NC*
*336-372-3400*

*Vera Brown serves up an order of her husband Doug's popular pork chops. Photo by Fred Sauceman.*

# BARBECUE AND BUTTERFAT

**JEFF SWOFFORD EXPERIENCED A CULINARY CONVERSION IN 2002.** His background was in the fast-food industry. He and his family once owned thirty-seven Hardee's restaurants in North Carolina and West Virginia.

From turning out rapid-fire burgers and fries, Jeff took an about-face as he opened the Brushy Mountain Smokehouse and Creamery in his hometown, North Wilkesboro, North Carolina. This former fast-food purveyor embraced one of the world's slowest cooking methods: barbecue. And he doesn't regret it for an instant.

Once dominated by demands for speedy service, Jeff Swofford's life now revolves around St. Louis-style ribs cooked for three hours and

*The barbecue at Brushy Mountain impressed Bobby Flay. Photo by Fred Sauceman.*

Boston butts cooked for fourteen and a half in a Southern Pride smoker with hickory wood.

This restaurant in the heart of the Piedmont takes an ecumenical attitude when it comes to North Carolina barbecue. Brushy Mountain's owners look to the eastern part of the state for their barbecue sauce inspiration. The house-made, glass-bottled sauce is dominated by vinegar, with only a hint of sweetness.

When asked to map the restaurant's barbecue, catering manager Daniel Harrison simply says, "It's Brushy Mountain Smokehouse style." And an element of that style is care.

"We hand-pull all our pork," adds Jeff. "It doesn't touch a blade."

Jeff and his coworkers not only look across the state for inspiration; they have also created an appetizer that combines a south-of-the-border staple with North Carolina meat and sauce. It's called the Barbecue Cruncher, and in addition to serving it as a sample to curious food writers, Daniel says it's a perfect way to introduce young children to barbecue. It consists of hickory-smoked pork butt stuffed inside a flour tortilla and deep-fried, with the vinegary barbecue sauce on the side.

In the tradition-bound business of barbecue, Jeff Swofford is an innovator. For another menu offering, he looks about as far east in North Carolina as you can go. The Saturday before Father's Day, the Swofford family heads for Holden Beach. There, Jeff got the idea to start serving shrimp burgers, and he added them to his menu in late 2012.

"Our shrimp burgers are loaded with Calabash shrimp," he says from a table in his restaurant some 290 miles from the ocean. Like most everything else on the menu, shrimp burgers are a common target for Brushy Mountain sauce.

Among the restaurant's side dish choices is more geographical diversity: a mayonnaise-bound slaw akin to those found in East Tennessee alongside a tart red barbecue slaw of Piedmont lineage. Both green and baked beans, corn nuggets made from creamed corn fried in batter, and baked cinnamon apples are oft-requested sides. Some of those apples fill traditional Southern fried pies, dusted with cinnamon sugar.

Although the worlds of chain fast food and slow-cooked barbecue are decidedly different, at Brushy Mountain, there is one common bond: ice cream. The Swofford family was the first to serve Hershey's ice cream in a Hardee's, and the pairing of barbecue and ice cream has been a trademark of Brushy Mountain from the start.

*The Barbecue Cruncher.*
*Photo by Fred Sauceman.*

Just inside the front door is a rainbow-hued case of house-made ice cream. As Jeff, his son Paul, and his cousin Todd were getting ready to open Brushy Mountain, they considered putting the barbecue cooker up front. Instead, that position was saved for the ice cream case. Jeff says thinking about the smell of waffle cones cooking sealed his decision.

There is a constantly evolving color palette of ice cream, with eighteen to twenty flavors at one time. Brushy Mountain Mud Pie is a blend of chocolate, coffee flavor, Oreos, and chocolate chips. Red velvet is a big seller, as is coconut. Jennifer Foster makes them all, and her ice cream repertoire is ever expanding. A customer once suggested a Krispy Kreme doughnut flavor. Two days later, Jennifer was stirring chopped doughnuts into cream. Jeff says when a customer suggests a new flavor and it is adopted, that customer gets the first quart free.

"Our ice cream is fourteen percent butterfat," Jennifer proclaims proudly. "We add French custard, and this machine takes all the air out of the product. Ice cream makes everybody smile."

But ask Jeff Swofford what he's most proud of at his restaurant, and he skips right over the knockout ribs and the ethereal ice cream. "Family," he answers without hesitation.

"All these servers, they've been here seven years or more. Nobody leaves. What I've enjoyed most are the relationships we've built. I've watched a ton of kids who worked here graduate from high school."

"Family" is a fitting theme for the Brushy Mountain Smokehouse and Creamery. The Swoffords are storied in North Carolina. Jeff's uncle John is Commissioner of the Atlantic Coast Conference. And then there is the late William Oliver Swofford—"Bill" to his family, "Oliver" to the world. Mounted on the wall in the Heritage Room is one of the hottest records of the 1960s, "Good Morning Starshine." Oliver released it in 1969, and it sold a million copies.

Yes, Brushy Mountain exhibits a "Starshine" record and a moonshine still, placed in the restaurant by longtime Swofford family friend and NASCAR legend Junior Johnson.

Walk along the walls of the restaurant, ice cream cone in hand, and you quickly absorb the history of Wilkes County: the floods of 1916 and 1940, the influence of Holly Farms Chicken (now Tyson), the prolific apple orchards, the heritage of North Wilkesboro Speedway, and Merle-Fest, the annual musical celebration memorializing the late son of the late North Carolina guitarist Doc Watson.

Along with those plates of smoked meat and cones of cold ice cream, the old photographs on the walls are a sign. They tell every Brushy Mountain Smokehouse and Creamery customer that the Swofford family respects the past and appreciates this place called Wilkes County. And those may be the best barbecue ingredients of all.

This story first appeared in *Our State* magazine in August 2013.

Brushy Mountain
Smokehouse and Creamery
201 Wilkesboro Boulevard
North Wilkesboro NC
336-667-9464

*Ham is really Ella Mae's last name. She has managed Shatley Springs for over 35 years. Photo by Fred Sauceman.*

# RUTABAGAS!

**"IT'S JUST COUNTRY COOKING," DECLARES ELLA MAE HAM,** who has managed the Shatley Springs Inn for more than thirty-five years. The bountiful side dishes served in the style of a boarding house largely reflect the traditional cooking of the North Carolina mountains.

Mashed potatoes, creamed corn, pinto beans, baked apples, turnip greens, green beans, and boiled cabbage are to be expected. The surprise?

Rutabagas. The root vegetable is more popular in Scandinavia than the United States. But Lee McMillan, who has owned Shatley Springs in Crumpler, North Carolina, since 1958, insists on them every day.

At Shatley, rutabagas are cooked with ham hocks. As are pinto beans. As is cabbage.

"We added rutabagas a couple of years ago, and people love them," says the aptly named Mrs. Ham.

Since around 1890, visitors to Martin Shatley's former farm have drunk and bathed in the spring's waters, claiming relief from skin diseases, stomach ailments, rheumatism, and "nervous disorders."

An equally compelling draw nowadays is the inn's family-style food, from fried chicken and country ham to a finale of banana pudding.

Shatley Springs Inn
407 Shatley Springs Road
Crumpler NC
336-982-2236

# CAROLINA PRIDE IN SPRUCE PINE

**THE UNDULATING AWNING AT THE CITY DRIVE-IN** is one of the most recognizable structures in Spruce Pine, North Carolina. Since 1950, diners have parked their cars under that blue wave, where curb hops continue to serve chili-smothered hamburgers and foot-long hot dogs. The City Drive-In remains a weekend hangout for western North Carolinians, with local bands performing live music every Friday and Saturday night.

Order a City Burger all the way, and you get it dressed with mustard, chili, slaw, and onion. The eight-hour chili recipe is the same as it was on the drive-in's opening day. Coleslaw is house-made as well.

City Drive-In hot dogs are, fittingly, supplied by Carolina Pride. The consensus among the City Drive-In staff is that deep-fried is the way to go.

Saturday mornings mean sausage gravy seasoned with bacon grease, made in the large black-iron skillet that owner Mike Long's mother once used to feed her seven children.

"It's just like I remember" is a common sentiment among former Spruce Pine residents who return for a memory of their childhood. Many marriages had their genesis under that blue awning.

*The City Drive-In*
*670 Oak Avenue*
*Spruce Pine NC*
*828-765-4480*

BUTTERMILK &
BIBLE BURGERS

*The undulating awning.*
*Photo by Fred Sauceman.*

# A CULINARY CONVERGENCE

**EDWARD YUZIUK, SON OF UKRAINIAN IMMIGRANTS, MOVED TO BURNSVILLE,** North
Carolina, in 1968 and started the town's newspaper, the *Yancey Journal*.
After he sold the newspaper, he opened the Garden Deli in 1987 on the
town square. Edward died in 1997, but the restaurant continued under
the ownership of his son, Greg, and Greg's wife, Hiroko. The Yuziuk
family's "totally secret" sauerkraut recipe traveled from Ukraine to Manhattan's East Village, where Edward grew up, and Edward's Japanese
daughter-in-law now makes it for Garden Deli pastrami Reuben sandwiches.

"Our bread is authentic New York rye, the same bread that is used by
the Carnegie Deli," Greg says.

As an economics student at the University of North Carolina in
Chapel Hill, Greg enjoyed the Greek grilled cheese sandwich served by

*Edward Yuziuk in 1974.
He would look out the
window of his newspaper
office in Burnsville,
North Carolina, and
dream about opening a
deli that sold the kinds of
sandwiches he grew up
with in New York. Photo
courtesy Greg Yuziuk.*

Hector's on Franklin Street, so he added it to the Garden Deli menu. Melted American cheese is seasoned with oregano. The sandwich is packed with lettuce, tomato, and onions and served on lightly grilled pita bread, with the Greek cucumber sauce, *tzatziki*.

"The pita is handmade and hand-stretched," says Greg. "We use Old World supplies."

Greg says his father "showed me everything" about the food business. That knowledge has been shared with Hiroko, who makes about eighty pounds of chicken salad every week and plates it up in four-ounce servings.

In the hands of the Yuziuk family, food traditions of Ukraine, Japan, Manhattan, and North Carolina converge on the well-laden plates at the Garden Deli.

*The Garden Deli*
*107 Town Square*
*Burnsville NC*
*828-682-3946*

BUTTERMILK &
BIBLE BURGERS

# THE OKRA AND CORNMEAL AFFINITY

**CONSIDER GRITS WITH GOAT CHEESE. CONTEMPLATE FRIED OKRA.** Those dishes illustrate what the Tupelo Honey Café in Asheville, North Carolina, is all about: innovation on an old Southern theme on the one hand coupled with the realization that the affinity between okra and cornmeal is eternal.

Come to the table at Tupelo and a hot biscuit soon follows, along with a squeeze bottle of the precious north Florida honey for which the place is named.

The Tupelo Honey Café is a bustling bastion of traditional and emerging Southern food in a city with a wealth of locally owned eateries.

*Nothing says Southern any better than okra fried in cornmeal. Photo by Fred Sauceman.*

*Tupelo Honey's Southern
Fried Chicken Saltimbocca
with Country Ham and
Mushroom Marsala.
Photo by Fred Sauceman.*

Of Tupelo's Southern Fried Chicken Saltimbocca with Country Ham and Mushroom Marsala, Chef Brian Sonoskus says, "I've always loved the Italian classic Saltimbocca, and I wanted to put my own Southern-inspired twist on it by frying the chicken and using North Carolina country ham instead of prosciutto. The classic version features sage. I switched it up further by using basil."

Additional proof of Tupelo's all-encompassing approach to Southern food and drink is a cocktail, Ode to Muddy Pond. It's a four-state salute to Southern ingredients: sorghum produced by the Guenther family in Tennessee, Maker's Mark bourbon from Kentucky, and spicy Blenheim ginger ale from South Carolina, blended in a North Carolina bar.

Tupelo Honey Café
12 College Street
Asheville NC
828-255-4863

# A NEW ROLE FOR THE HUSHPUPPY

**THINGS CHANGED AT THE PISGAH FISH CAMP** the day a customer crumbled hush-puppies over spiced apples. The savory take on apple crisp caught on. Hushpuppies, of course, have always been typical fish camp fare, going back to the days when newspapers covered tables.

At this Transylvania County, North Carolina, restaurant, spiced apples have a history, too. The dish was created by the late Nadine Thomas, who worked the fish fryers in the Pisgah Fish Camp kitchen for thirty-five years. In fact, owner Dana Hawkins says Thomas "perfected" spiced apples, their color resembling the flesh of pink grapefruit.

*Local trout, house-made hushpuppies, and a former employee's recipe for cooked apples. Photo by Fred Sauceman.*

*Double-dipped onion rings.*
*Photo by Fred Sauceman.*

The Pisgah Fish Camp opened in 1967. Dana's father Dan moved from managing a dime store to a bowling alley to a restaurant. "We're now seeing the third generation come through here," says Dana.

Considering the variety of fish and seafood and the options for preparing them, Pisgah offers diners more than 1,000 different choices.

A mandatory meal starter is a basket of peppery onion rings. "We use colossal yellow onions and hand-bread them in a special salt and pepper breading, not a typical batter," says Dana. "They're actually double-dipped. We go through a couple of hundred pounds of onions a week."

Dining at the Pisgah Fish Camp, you get the feeling that there's nothing this former Western Carolina University student would rather be doing than frying fish for his friends at the family business. The rewards, he says, are "instantaneous."

*The Pisgah Fish Camp*
*140 New Hendersonville Hwy*
*Pisgah Forest NC*
*828-877-3129*

BUTTERMILK &
BIBLE BURGERS

# BREAKFAST ON THE OCONALUFTEE

**THE MEAL IS FILLING. THE VIEW IS STUNNINGLY BEAUTIFUL.** Diners at Peter's Pancakes and Waffles in Cherokee, North Carolina, often pass up immediate seating to wait for a table next to the windows in the back. Behind the restaurant flows the Oconaluftee River, bordered by a purple-flowering Royal Paulownia tree.

"I'll get about ten questions a week about the identity of that tree," says manager Dwight Ryals.

Peter's is a laminated menu kind of place, with a huge array of waffle and pancake choices. Options range from a plain, syrup-topped buckwheat pancake to a strawberry-and-whipped-cream-crowned Belgian-style

*From plain to buckwheat to Belgian, pancakes and waffles are all-day fare at Peter's. Photo by Fred Sauceman.*

*Diners often turn down more immediate seating for a table overlooking the river at Peter's Pancakes and Waffles. Photo by Fred Sauceman.*

waffle. The restaurant is located within the Qualla Boundary and is Native American-owned.

For even bigger appetites, Huevos Enrique combines sweet peppers, onions, sausage, diced potatoes, eggs, pepper Jack cheese, sour cream, and a side of jalapeños.

The mallard ducks nearby have caught on to the goodness at Peter's. Dwight Ryals says they walk right up to the kitchen door expecting biscuit and toast crumbs. During winter, it's not unusual to see half a dozen elk exploring the river. And diners who can't wait on a river view enjoy watching groundhogs cavort on the hillside across Tsali Boulevard.

Fortified with a satisfying breakfast and inspired by wildlife, water, and mountain, you understand deep inside the passion of the Cherokees for this part of the world.

*Peter's Pancakes
and Waffles
1384 Tsali Boulevard
Cherokee NC
828-497-5116*

# NINETEENTH-CENTURY DINING

**"WHAT WOULD YOU FOLKS LIKE TO DRINK, SWEET TEA?"** asks the server, in a way that leads you to believe the choice is obvious. And it is. Hot biscuits and honey follow.

Boardinghouse-style food has been served at The Jarrett House in Dillsboro, North Carolina, since 1884. Owners Jean and Jim Hartbarger say the menu is largely unchanged from that era: fried chicken, mountain-cured country ham, buttered potatoes, candied apples, green beans, pickled beets, and chicken and dumplings.

The Jarrett House has been in the capable hands of the Hartbargers for around forty years. Eight members of the family work there. Jim is a

BUTTERMILK & BIBLE BURGERS

*The Jarrett House in Dillsboro, North Carolina, has been feeding folks since the presidency of Chester Alan Arthur. Photo by Fred Sauceman.*

former basketball coach at Western Carolina University. Jean taught kindergarten and first grade. For eight years, she was Dillsboro's mayor, and she is an authority on the history of the tiny town.

"We had no idea what we were getting into," she says, laughing as she recalls the abrupt career changes, moving from education to the hospitality business.

When the Hartbargers bought The Jarrett House, Jean says, "A lot of the older cooks were still here."

She learned from them, and she preserved dishes like vinegar pie, an everyday offering at The Jarrett House. The contradictory-sounding title puzzles some diners, Jean says. To clear up the confusion, she compares the dessert to chess pie.

"But during and after the Civil War, lemons were hard to come by, so vinegar was substituted as the acidic ingredient," Jean theorizes.

In 1936, Duncan Hines published the first edition of his restaurant guidebook, *Adventures in Good Eating.* The Jarrett House is one of a handful of places covered by Hines that still survive.

 ## Jarrett House Vinegar Pie

1   stick margarine, melted and cooled

1 1/2 cups sugar

2   tablespoons flour

1   tablespoon vanilla

2   tablespoons apple cider vinegar

3   eggs

1   9-inch unbaked pie shell

*Combine the 6 ingredients.*

*Our cooks say to beat the eggs well before adding the rest of the ingredients.*

*Pour into the unbaked pie shell. Bake at 300 degrees for 45 minutes.*

# SMOKING IN HOTHOUSE

**THE COMMUNITY IS CALLED HOTHOUSE. THE ADDRESS IS MURPHY.** But that's misleading. The building sits some fifteen miles west of the North Carolina town, in the state's far southwestern corner. To Tennessee, it's four and a half miles. To Georgia, it's three.

Herb's Pit Bar-B-Que is almost all alone. There's not another business in sight. Vaughn Gibson, Herb's son, says the family was "crazy to build a restaurant on this spot."

But the Gibsons have beaten the odds. Folks throughout this tri-state area knew of Herb Gibson's reputation with a rack of ribs. He fed fellow

*Dave Gibson built this pit using brick from an old copper mine in Tennessee. Photo by Fred Sauceman.*

copper miners over in Ducktown and Copperhill, in Tennessee. His sons remember whole pigs cooked on holidays.

Herb has always had a devilish sense of humor. After his mining career, he named his first restaurant The Sahara, a reference to the devastation of the landscape and the lack of greenery caused by copper mining and sulfuric acid production.

In 1982, Herb decided to parlay his reputation as a barbecue man into a business, Herb's Pit Bar-B-Que. For the pit, son Dave salvaged brick from an old copper mine.

"I never had laid brick," Dave tells me as we check the progress of that evening's ribs. "I priced bricklayers and then decided to do it myself. Built the whole pit."

Barbecue at Herb's has always been fueled by native hickory, along with charcoal. Never a canister of gas or a volt of electricity.

"It's charcoal for heat, hickory for flavor," says Dave, who has tended that homemade pit for more than thirty years now. "An open pit is very unforgiving. Too hot, and you burn the meat. Not hot enough, it won't even cook. In the wintertime you're fighting the elements. Every thirty minutes you're adding to that fire."

The ribs that come off that fire, says Vaughn, don't taste "stewed or boiled." They're finished with a "broiler sauce," which is the restaurant's sweet and sour barbecue sauce thickened down, forming a glaze on the meat. No "rib rub" is used.

Pork butt comes to the table sauced and chopped. Pork loin is served sliced and sauced.

"Most people don't use loins," Vaughn says. "They can dry out too easily." Close control over the cooking temperature and a sauce bath keep that from happening.

Herb and Helen Gibson and their two sons understand the nuances of regional barbecue. They walk the lines of demarcation in the barbecue world very carefully.

"In Georgia, people like a tomatoey, sweet sauce. Here in North Carolina, the preference is vinegary and a little sweet. Our sauce is sweet and sour," proclaims Vaughn diplomatically.

A second sauce, appropriately served in a red bottle, is flavored with habanero and jalapeño peppers.

Listed at the top of the menu at Herb's is the BBQ Feast: ribs, a quarter of a chicken, sliced BBQ, BBQ Polish kielbasa, baked beans, slaw, potato salad, and rolls or hushpuppies. Below it is the BBQ Sampler, which includes, as the menu states, "all of the above, but a little less so we don't have to wheel you out."

Most every element of the business at Herb's Pit Bar-B-Que speaks of tradition. Among the predictable side dishes is one unexpected, listed as both an appetizer and a side: onion rings.

"Restaurant people generally don't like to make them," Vaughn says, "but they have been on the menu at Herb's since we opened the doors."

The batter is crisp and light, almost like a Japanese tempura.

"When my boys were growing up, we had kids at our house all the time," remembers Helen. "They could eat those onion rings faster than I could make them."

Another gem from the Helen Gibson kitchen has also been on the menu at Herb's since the beginning. Call it choco-

*It's a lonely-looking location, but crowds converge from three states to partake of barbecue at Herb's, near Murphy, North Carolina. Photo by Fred Sauceman.*

late pie, and Helen is quick to point out that it isn't served in wedges, and there's no meringue topping. Helen's take on chocolate pie involves a cookie-like crust, a cream cheese layer, a chocolate layer, whipped cream on top, all striped with chocolate. She calls it a Four-Layer Chocolate Pie, and even those who have polished off the BBQ Feast have been known to save room for it.

Family togetherness and respect for tradition have shepherded this restaurant through radical changes in the regional economy. Herb's former livelihood, copper mining, is gone. Plants like Levi Strauss & Co. have shut down. Herb's Pit Bar-B-Que has survived it all.

In addition to a strong local clientele from the three states, Herb's relies on tourism to keep the business viable. Flowing rivers and falling leaves make April to November 1 the peak season for travelers in this part of North Carolina. The restaurant is only a short distance from the Ocoee River, one of the nation's most popular destinations for whitewater rafting. The area gained worldwide exposure in 1996 when the Olympic slalom canoe and kayak events took place in the Ocoee River Gorge.

BUTTERMILK &
BIBLE BURGERS

Herb's Pit Bar-B-Que
Highway 64 West
Murphy NC
828-494-5367

As the economy evolved, so did Herb's. Ribeye steaks, prime rib, shrimp, catfish, and mountain trout were added to the weekend menu to accommodate the tastes of an expanding clientele. But, Vaughn says, "We have held on to what made us. We still cook barbecue over an open fire, with a fire box, even though it's smoky, nasty, hard work."

I ask Vaughn about the rewards that make all that labor worthwhile. "We enjoy people talking about our food, saying we've done a good job. From our dad, we learned that you should try to do a good job at everything you do. He always said that kids shouldn't have idle time on their hands."

Advancing age keeps Herb from attending to the barbecue business every day as he once did. But his visage, in a black-and-white photograph taken by an employee, overlooks the gift shop and reception area that his son Dave built with his own hands.

Dave says the photographer captured his father's mischievous personality perfectly. In that picture, Herb is holding a pair of tongs—symbolic of the "tending to," of the attention, care, and never-ending manual labor that the Gibson family has generously devoted to customers from near and far for more than three decades.

This story first appeared in *Our State* magazine in April 2013.

# CINCINNATI STEAK
# AND CHERRY SMASH IN SOUTH CAROLINA

**THE THURMAN BURGER OF COLUMBUS, OHIO, IS KNOWN FOR ITS HEIGHT.** The defining characteristic of a Guberburger at the Wheel Inn of Sedalia, Missouri, is a smear of heated peanut butter. At Solly's Grille in Milwaukee, Wisconsin, hamburgers are capped with gobs of butter. Paul Duberek steams "cheeseburgs," and the cheese, too, at Ted's Restaurant in Meriden, Connecticut.

Writer George Motz traversed the country in search of hamburgers and published his findings in *Hamburger America: A State-By-State Guide to 100 Great Burger Joints*, a book with a companion DVD. Some states

*A Northgate hamburger topped with molten pimento cheese. Photo by Fred Sauceman.*

didn't make the cut. Apparently Motz didn't find a burger to his liking in West Virginia, since that state isn't represented in the book at all. Also absent is Alabama. California tops the list with nine joints featured, followed by Texas with eight.

There are four entries from Tennessee: Brown's Diner in Nashville; Dyer's in Memphis; Rotier's Restaurant in Nashville; and Zarzour's Café in Chattanooga.

The management at Dyer's claims to cook hamburgers in grease that hasn't been changed since 1912. Zarzour's, despite its Middle-Eastern lineage, is a Southern meat and vegetable emporium.

Virginia merits one entry in Motz's book: Roanoke's Texas Tavern, home of the Cheesy Western, a burger dressed with a fried egg and cabbage relish.

Motz's only South Carolina selection is the Northgate Soda Shop in Greenville. Originally a drugstore with prepackaged sandwiches, Northgate, when it came under the ownership of Jim DeYoung in 1965, helped define a South Carolina tradition: hamburgers smeared with pimento cheese.

Northgate's pimento cheese is scratch-made, with sharp cheddar, Greenville's own Duke's mayonnaise, and pimentos. Once the hamburger is halfway cooked, it's flipped and topped with the pimento cheese.

"It's different, unique, not something you can order at McDonald's, Burger King, or any of the chains," says Northgate's manager Brenda Vaughan, a native South Carolinian and a graduate of Wofford College. "We leave the pimento cheese on there long enough to start the melting process, but it still has enough firmness to hold itself together on the sandwich. We don't pulverize the cheese into a spread. It's still chunky cheddar, shredded cheddar, and holds that form."

Joining the Pimento Cheeseburger on Northgate's menu is the Cincinnati Steak Sandwich—sliced deli bologna, fried and topped with chili and cheese. It's patterned after another South Carolina specialty, a hamburger covered in chili.

Actress Catherine Christophillis owns the Northgate now. On Thursdays, the "theatre crowd" comes in. The Chris Evans Burger got its name because one of the actors kept ordering a bacon cheeseburger with a fried egg on top.

Steve Green from Travelers Rest stocks the Northgate in fried pies. Cheriee Esteve bakes twelve-layer chocolate cakes and Kentucky pound cakes for sale at the counter.

During the forty-one years he owned the place, Jim DeYoung accumulated an amazing collection of church and funeral home fans, which he left in place when he sold the business. And not only church and funeral home fans but also ones promoting Lutheran Homes, the Furman Paladins, Miss Greenville, the musical group Southern Culture on the Skids, the South Carolina Gamecocks, Clemson University, and the University of Georgia Bulldogs.

Brenda points out two curious photographs behind the counter. The shot of James Brown shaking hands with the Pope, she says, is an "unusual pairing. They don't sound like they go together in the same sentence."

The other photograph she shows us is almost as strange. The late South Carolina senator Strom Thurmond sits on a lifeguard chair surrounded by women in bathing suits.

Situated next to the Northgate Laundry & Cleaners and easy to overlook, the soda shop opened in 1947 and still serves fountain drinks typical of that era, plus some new versions. Cherry syrup and soda water make a Cherry Smash. With a Pimento Cheeseburger, Brenda recommends an Orangeade, made with the freshly squeezed juices of oranges, lemons, and limes.

*Northgate Soda Shop*
*918 North Main Street*
*Greenville SC*
*864-235-6770*

"The fountain has several dispensers," she told us. "We have chocolate, cherry, strawberry, and vanilla syrups, and we can add them to any drink. We make Cherry Pepsis, even Chocolate Pepsis."

Despite being heralded by George Motz as one of America's top 100 burger joints, Northgate Soda Shop goes about its unpretentious way, delighting a largely local clientele by serving a South Carolina signature: hamburgers crowned with pimento cheese.

# AN AFTERWORD

**IN OUR DINING ROOM IN TENNESSEE,** near that watercolor painting of Trula Bailey and her whole wheat muffins, sits one of our most treasured possessions. It's a teapot, handmade in Mobile, Alabama, in 1970 by Lyn Johnson as a tribute to my grandmother, Edith Ethel Koontz Royall, whose story and stuffed peppers are included in this book.

On one side of that teapot is the Wesley Blessing:

> Be Present at Our Table, Lord.
> Be Here and Everywhere Adored.
> These Mercies Bless and Grant That We
> May Feast in Paradise with Thee.

On the other side is what we called Grandmother's Blessing:

> God is Great and God is Good.
> Let Us Thank Him for Our Food.
> By His Grace We All Are Fed.
> Give Us Lord, Our Daily Bread.

Grandmother Royall relearned both these blessings after a devastating stroke that nearly killed her. Throughout her life, despite a series of hardships, she never complained. She quietly kept on. She persisted. And she prevailed. Although she died in 1971, her spirit remains a guiding influence in my life. That teapot is a symbol of the gratitude she had for the gifts she had been given. She realized that food is both earthly and eternal. This lesson, passed down to me, is an inheritance that has shaped my life in ways my grandmother could have never imagined.

In my part of the world, in Appalachia, hearing blessings like these at meals is still common, I am happy to report. I chose to include them not at the beginning of this book, however, but at the end, as prelude to the next meal, the next relationship, the next connection still to come, around a table or inside a kitchen, somewhere on the open road.

*The two-blessing teapot. Photo by Fred Sauceman.*

# INDEX

BUTTERMILK &
BIBLE BURGERS

**BUTTERMILK &
BIBLE BURGERS**

191

BUTTERMILK &
BIBLE BURGERS